# Early Years Play

3657

P. 11.

# Early Years Play

## A Happy Medium for Assessment and Intervention

**Zahirun Sayeed and Ellen Guerin**

**David Fulton Publishers**
London

David Fulton Publishers Ltd
Ormond House, 26–27 Boswell Street, London WC1N 3JD

Web site: http://www.fultonbooks.co.uk

First published in Great Britain by David Fulton Publishers 2000

Note: The right of Zahirun Sayeed and Ellen Guerin to be identified as the authors of this work has been asserted by them in accordance with the Copyright, Designs and Patents Act 1988.

*British Library Cataloguing in Publication Data*

A catalogue record for this book is available from the British Library

ISBN 1–85346–662–X

Typeset by FiSH Books, London
Printed in Great Britain by The Cromwell Press Ltd, Trowbridge, Wilts.

# Contents

## Dedications

To Kevin Hassett, a sadly missed key-player.

Ellen


To Shopon, who continues to play in his adulthood.
To Farah, Sadat and Sarah, who reminded me
how to play.

Runi

# Foreword

I am delighted to welcome this book as a contribution to debate and practice on assessment and intervention.

Both Zahirun Sayeed and Ellen Guerin are experienced teachers and educational psychologists who between them have worked with many children of all ages. They have specially developed an interest and expertise in early years play-based assessment and have already written on this topic. This text provides them with the opportunity to expand and describe their ideas and practices, for a wider audience.

Their philosophy is rooted in the rights and entitlements of all young children to equitable assessment that fairly gives them the opportunity to show their developing skills and areas of potential – in other words, 'a fair play' approach. The application of these ideas will be relevant to practitioners working in a range of early years settings, as well as to early years policy makers, advisers, educational psychologists and to those charged with the responsibility of training early years staff.

I consider that this book makes a distinctive contribution. It encompasses the realms of play, assessment and intervention and weaves these into a convincing theoretical formulation which has direct implications for those who work with all young children. The emphasis upon close cooperation between all the adults who have significant responsibilities for young children reflects contemporary views as to how *inclusive* approaches can work in practice.

Sheila Wolfendale
University of East London
March 2000

# Acknowledgements

We would like to record our gratitude to all those who helped us so generously in completing this book. Particular thanks to Professor Sheila Wolfendale for writing the Foreword. Thanks to Jane Calliste and Abu Sayeed for exercising their proof-reading skills and Sadat Sayeed for IT support. Thanks to the staff and parents of Columbia Market Nursery, Tower Hamlets, London who were unfailingly courteous and helpful in supporting our research and photographs. Thanks to our colleagues at Tower Hamlets Educational Psychology Service for their encouragement and goodwill. We are grateful to the educational psychologists in training who participated in our research.

We both express our gratitude to our friends and family for their patience and reassurance throughout the period of research and writing.

# Preface

This book aims to describe the process of working with young children, researching and writing on the subject of play in the context of practising Educational Psychology. The authors recognise the need to address the role and status of play for all young children in a range of settings: home, nursery, playgroup, etc. The extensive literature and conflicting perspectives on play challenged the authors' understanding and formulation of their own views of play, raising as many questions as answers. While exploring the theory and practice of play, the transience, abundance and vastness of an ocean became a useful metaphor. The authors felt like scuba divers, realising their scope within a limitless space with plentiful resources and varied activities.

In the first chapter the authors endeavour to introduce the general concept of play by exploring the meaning and attributes of play from the literature. Existing knowledge is analysed and structured for the reader, thus enabling the authors to refine their own definition of play.

Various theoretical frameworks, from past to present day, are summarised in Chapter 2 in the following categories: Historical, Behaviour, Learning, Expression, Education, Chaology, Interaction and Process. The *Interactionist perspective* advocated by the authors is elaborated, providing a basis for later suggestions for play-providers around policy and practice.

In the third chapter, the authors ask whether play is culture-free or culture-biased. Research and practice around cultural influences on play refer to race, gender and ethnicity. Within this brief, themes such as parental expectations, the status of play, the availability of play provision and the link between play and work across cultures are highlighted. At an ideological level the 'child's right to play' is vehemently promoted and at a practical level it is made clear that the child's ability, race, colour and nationality need to be considered and understood.

The close association between a child's play and emotional development is the main focus of Chapter 4. Case examples are used as illustrations and emphasis is placed on the relationship between changes within the child and in the context where he/she plays. The developmental nature of thought, emotion and empathy in relation to play is discussed. The benefits of a playful disposition for the young learner and the therapeutic nature of play are recognised by parents and professionals.

With direct reference to the *Code of Practice on the Identification and Assessment of Special Educational Needs* (DfE 1994) in Chapter 5 the authors make a case for the relevance of play for children with SEN. The *inclusive nature of play* is illustrated through carefully selected examples (based on the author's experience) and with reference to the current research. The concept of Individual Education Planning is extended to *Individual Play Plans* (IPP) with an emphasis on adult participation and interaction during a child's play.

The authors' revised model of *Play-Based Assessment* (PBA) in Chapter 6 is at the heart of the book. The background to and development of this model is described. In addition to the presentation of the model of PBA, it contains a schedule for background information, assessment prompt-sheets and a summary sheet to support planning. The PBA model strongly advocates that the child's development and learning is assessed through appropriate adult observation and participation during play.

The seventh chapter highlights how children's play can be enhanced through social interaction. Vygotsky's and Feuerstein's theories form the basis of the authors' understanding of the child's potential for play, thinking and learning and the role of the adult as a mediator.

In Chapter 8 the authors attempt to 'bridge the gap' between assessment and intervention through the medium of play. Dynamic Assessment (DA) provides an alternative to other conventional forms of assessment discussed, in particular, as it embodies simultaneous intervention. The link between DA and PBA is outlined and the concept of *Mediated Play Experience* (MPE) is introduced with case examples.

The final thoughts chapter enables the authors to reflect upon the process and product of their 'dive' into the realm of play with ideas for consideration by significant adults responsible for children's play and learning.

Zahirun Sayeed and Ellen Guerin
London
March 2000

## Chapter 1

# They're only playing

**Figure 1.1** They're only playing

Man only plays when he is in the fullest sense of the word a human being
and he is only a fully human being when he plays.

Schiller (in Sutton-Smith 1985. p.64)

The word 'play' conjures up images of laughter, enjoyment, indulgence and
sharing. For adults play is an optional and conscious activity where leisure-time
is used to balance the trials and tribulations of everyday modern living. In the case
of children play is an essential and integral part of their existence which

constitutes a right. If it is accepted that play is central to the life of a child then as adults we must ask how well we understand play, and how much we value play for our children. Although much has been written on the subject of children's play this anomaly continues to pose challenges for parents, professionals and wider society that generally recognise its importance but struggle to find a place for play. The authors will endeavour to explore the meaning of children's play and locate it in a context where it can be valued and understood.

## Views of play

It is generally known that children's play permeates the boundaries of race, colour, language, religion and culture, but if this the case what is to be understood by this enigmatic concept? The Oxford English Dictionary very simply defines play as occupying oneself in a game or other recreational activities. Early definitions are as relevant today as they were in the past. In his book *Homoludens*, Huizinga (1949) described play as a voluntary activity or occupation executed within fixed limits of time and place, having its aim in itself and accompanied by a feeling of joy and consciousness that is 'different' from ordinary life. His definition usefully outlines the purpose, process and product of play. Deardon (1967 p. 84) emphasises the emotional benefit of play for the child. 'Play is a non-serious and self-contained activity which we engage in just for the satisfaction involved in it'. Matterson (1975) extends this idea to describe how a child learns what no one else can teach him/her. She describes play as providing a context where the world is presented in a manageable form where quantities are controlled. Play can include fictional situations and relationships with others where learning can take place. Christie (1991) attaches more value to the process of play than the product. Play behaviours are described as flexible, creative, voluntary and pleasurable. They must be self-motivated and focus on means rather than ends and are at times abstract.

From the literature it quickly becomes apparent that the concept of childhood play varies enormously. Research is based largely on observations of the players (children) by non-players (adults) as the players are not generally expected to be able to describe what they are/were doing while they are/were engaging in play. Indeed the complexities of play as evident from the rules, sanctions, exceptions and adaptations made by children in the play situation are prone to misinterpretation by adult onlookers. As in every situation, observers are prone to interpretations based in their own attitudes, thoughts, memories and experiences. For adult observers there is often the sense that if one is not a player then one cannot really understand the dynamics of the play situation. In the words of Winnicott (1971 p. 60), 'the child inhabits an area that cannot be easily left nor can it easily admit intrusions'. This makes the role of the adult observing or participating in a child's play a challenging one.

The contextualised nature of what constitutes play is confusing and misleading. Play can take place anywhere (home, school, on the street, in the local playground, etc.). Essential to play is the child's feeling of security, a desire to play and the ability to play. Play materials are important but not essential for play to take place.

There are several discrepancies and contrasting views of play in the literature. Although a definition of play is important this does not mean that a single definition is necessary or easy to attain. It has been suggested that play should be viewed in terms of its attributes rather than an all-embracing definition but there is as much variation in the range of suggested attributes as differing definitions. However challenging, it does seem worthwhile to embrace the definitions, characteristics and types of play in order to provide the fullest picture of this phenomenon and offer the authors' perspective in these areas.

In the existing literature definitions of play tend to fall into two categories:

1. *What the child does and what changes take place within the child while playing.* Rubin *et al.* (1983) describe play as intrinsically motivated as opposed to being imposed or led by others. Play is concerned with the means and not the outcome. It is free from external rules and the child is engaged in a non-serious activity. Their views of play are process-led.
2. *What the child gets out of the play situation.* Isenberg and Jacobs (1982) defined play as children's work and how they learn about the world around them. Their view of play is product-led.

## Process-led descriptors of play

- Intrinsic motivation: The child engages voluntarily in the act of playing.
- Enjoyment: Play is a positive and pleasurable experience for the child.
- Learning: Play facilitates the learning process.
- Happiness: Play gratifies the child, fulfilling his/her emotional needs.
- Development: The child's level of development is demonstrated through play and his/her levels of functioning can be assessed and enhanced through play experiences.
- Interaction: Through play the child interacts with the environment including people and objects.
- Context/time/space: The play process occurs in a supportive environment and within limits of time and place.

## Product-led descriptors of play

- Thinking: Play offers an opportunity for the child to apply his/her existing thoughts and extend his/her thinking skills.
- Motor activity: Most play activities involve a child being physically active and use of his/her physical energy in order to develop skills for the future.

- Behaviour: Play is an observable response to stimuli such as play materials and activities.
- Preparation for the future: Play allows the child to develop skills and knowledge for later life.

In order to gauge an impression of views held by parents and professionals a short study was conducted by the authors in 1996, using a small sample of nursery staff and parents in Tower Hamlets, London. Their descriptions of play came under the following headings:

- Exploratory
- Communicative
- Enjoyable
- Sociable
- Educational
- Imaginative.

One member of nursery staff defined play as 'exploration – finding out about the world, practising skills in an exciting, stimulating and non-threatening environment'. In response to the question 'what do you mean by play?', a parent responded 'learning about the world and having fun'.

In 1999 a structured interview was administered to ten sets of parents of nursery children in order to ascertain their view of a child's play. When asked 'Tell me what you understand by children's play', responses such as using his/her imagination and enjoying him/herself were most commonly cited. Similarly when asked 'What does your child do when he/she plays?', 50 per cent of the parents referred to 'pretending' and 40 per cent referred to imitative play. The abstract and complex nature of children's play was very prevalent in the responses given and indicated high levels of awareness and sensitivity on the part of parents. However, as is the case among educationalists and other professionals, the types of play cited as play behaviours have different meanings for different people. This has direct implications for the kind of learning and development encouraged among children at home and in educational settings.

A small-scale study to elicit the views of educational psychologists in training was carried out during the authors' lecture visits to four UK training courses in 1998. Groups of two to four students, all of whom were ex-teachers with a minimum of two years of teaching experience, were given five to ten minutes to arrive at definitions of play. Their definitions included the following:

- 'A voluntary form of recreation in which an individual may develop cognitive, creative, social and emotional skills.'
- 'An active interaction with your environment and with others.'
- 'Play is an interactive exploration of the environment. It is self-motivating, absorbing, enjoyable and intrinsically rewarding. It can be a powerful medium for learning.'

- 'A process by which individuals are able to express themselves and develop a range of cognitive and social skills by interacting with their environment and/or other individuals.'
- 'Play is essential to healthy growth and development. It should be an enjoyable experience within which the child can learn through exploration and discovery, gaining a range of social, cognitive and physical skills.'
- 'Play is a fun way of learning life skills. It allows a child freedom of expression, a sense of control, modelling what they have seen, repeating favourite activities and elaborating their ideas.'
- 'An external representation of internal understanding of life experiences and the world.'
- 'Manifestation of inner world into external reality.'

The five most commonly cited attributes of play in the definitions were as follows:

**Table 1.1** Attributes of play within definitions

| Exploratory | Skill-enhancing |
|---|---|
| Enjoyable | Sociable |
| Educational | |

Interestingly, the definitions provided by this group have striking similarities with those offered by parents and nursery staff as well as the definitions available in the literature. Fundamentally this would suggest that there are common understandings of play but disparate descriptions do not seem to encompass play in its entirety.

In the authors' view, play can be defined in terms of its overt and assumed characteristics. A child's play is elicited in response to a person or object in a context where he/she feels secure. Over time the child expends physical and mental energy for pleasure through the application of skills such as improvisation and creativity. As a state, play assumes absorption, concentration and an escape to a world that the child creates for him/herself individually or as part of a group (Sayeed and Guerin 1997 p. 46).

The provision of a safe environment with adequate space and time is crucial to meaningful play.

## Attributes of play

Features of play are often cited in order to get around the difficulty of providing a neat, all-encompassing definition. The authors accord with Catherine Garvey (1991) who described the following attributes of play:

- Play is pleasurable and enjoyable
- Play has no extrinsic goal
- Play is spontaneous and voluntary
- Play involves some active engagement on the part of the player
- Play has certain systematic relations to what is not play including creativity, problem solving, language learning and the development of social roles.

Overall the attributes of play as outlined in the literature seem to be described in more specific, observable terms than the definitions. They tend to be either assumed or observed and include those in Table 1.2.

**Table 1.2** Assumed and observed attributes of play

| Assumed: | Observed: |
|---|---|
| Child's own agenda | Interactive |
| Enjoyable | Rule governed |
| Incorporates 'pretend' | Observable behaviour |
| Meets the emotional needs of child | Physical |
| Free flow/flexible in nature | Language-based |
| Involves thinking and concentration | Sequenced |
| Process-led | |
| Meaningful | |

An attributional approach provides a broader picture of play than a short definition can afford. However attributions need to be considered collectively as opposed to individually. The Rumbold Report (DES 1990) describes play as 'an essential and rich part of the learning process'. However a number of conditions have to be fulfilled:

- Sensitive knowledge and informed adult involvement and intervention.
- Careful planning and organisation of the play setting.
- Time for children to develop their play.
- Careful observation of children's activities to facilitate assessment and planning for progression and continuity.

This description of the context for play fits closely with that of the authors, who characterise quality play experiences in interactionist terms. According to the authors, play should be considered in relation to the child and context.

**Table 1.3** The child and a context for play

| The child must: | The context must be: |
| --- | --- |
| Feel secure | Safe |
| Follow his/her own agenda | Interactive |
| Enjoy him/herself | Inviting |
| Develop and learn | Sustaining |

The language of play in theory and practice is confusing and contradictory. The labelling of the types of play has been significantly affected by the use of objective terminology. Terms such as 'imaginative', 'fantasy' and 'pretend' have the same meaning for some and different meaning for others. For example, does 'pretend play' as described by Beardsley and Harnett (1998) mean the same as 'imaginative play' by Jeffree *et al.* (1979)? In conclusion, unless a type of play is linked closely to clear examples it is difficult to distinguish between what could be similar types of play. An overview of the current literature identifies six types of play, which are commonly known as exploratory, creative, imaginative, physical, problem solving and social. Tina Bruce (1991) identified free-flow play in which the child explores his/her environment in a random and complex way, testing his/her ideas, experimenting with his/her feelings and relationships while simultaneously developing skills and competence.

Free-flow play is 'wallowing in ideas, feelings and relationships and the application of competence mastery and technical prowess that has already been developed' (Bruce 1991 p. 4). Her idea is based on Gleick's Chaos Theory (1988) which will be further discussed in the next chapter in addition to other theoretical perspectives on play.

## Chapter 2

# Do we really understand children's play?

This chapter aims to further explore the concept of play in relation to various theoretical perspectives. Parents and professionals who work with children gather information and facts to further their understanding of play. However, the facts do not speak for themselves and are better understood when they are brought together and analysed in terms of an organised framework or theory. No single, unified theory can completely explain the significance of play in a child's development. However, an understanding of play can be derived from perspectives of developmental, cognitive, behavioural and social psychology as well as theories of education. These are based on established views and principles, which offer differing angles on play and provide a richer understanding of the meaning of play. An analysis of these perspectives has facilitated the authors' own rationale for explaining and using play in a particular way.

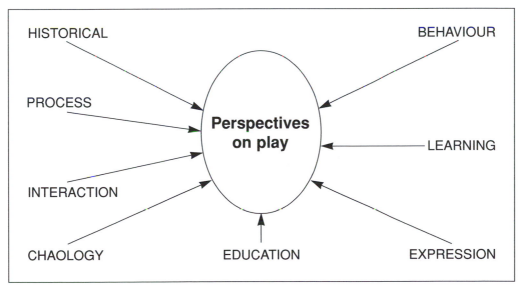

**Figure 2.1** Perspectives on play

## An historical context

The first theories of play were developed during the late nineteenth and early twentieth century. Until the nineteenth century childhood was viewed as an immature adulthood where the needs of children were not considered any different from those of adults.

Many early theorists of the time identified closely with Darwin's theory of evolution. Although they started to change how society viewed children they focused on simple comparisons between children and other species. Consequently they described play in contradictory, oversimplistic terms. Spencer (1878) described play as means of relaxation and a way to expend surplus energy without ulterior benefits. In his book *The Play of Men* (1901), Groos stated that play was the main purpose of childhood. He documented the link between play and learning and identified play as the practice of skills for survival and use in later adult life. In 1908, Hall's Recapitulation Theory of ancestral behaviour explored the idea that children repeat earlier stages of human evolution during their development and play provides a medium for their expression.

More recently these classical views of play have been criticised because they emphasise the functional characteristics of play and disregard the value of play as an enjoyable, worthwhile experience for the child. In the course of the twentieth century there has been a shift in thinking around childhood play. Play has become more child-centred and the benefits of play for development of the child have been emphasised.

## Play, behaviour and learning

What is a behaviour? A behaviour can be defined as an observable response to stimuli. Therefore if play is an observable response to a stimulus it should be categorised as behaviour. Play can be initiated though the introduction of a stimulus such as an object, preferred toy or activity and play behaviour is modified by experience and can be learned and generalised into other contexts. Skinner's Theory of Learning (1953) can be applied to a child's play. Play can be shaped and maintained through rewards when applied consistently and appropriately.

Later theorists such as Claxton (1984) argue that there is no one model of learning, i.e. we can only say what a person is learning by how he/she behaves. He describes the characteristics of a good learner as one who takes time, asks questions, is not afraid of getting things wrong and enjoys finding out. He equates play with learning and how the child's 'knowing' in a play situation gives him or her the confidence to know more.

Piaget (1962) viewed the child as a scientist who experiments with his/her own learning. His concept of play is clearly set within his theory of cognitive development (the development of thinking and learning). Problem solving was central to Piaget's view of play and he emphasised 'a continuity between a child's play and his work'. He saw play as a means by which the child combines existing skills, knowledge and understanding, resulting in learning experiences. He identified three stages and categories in the development of a child's play. According to Piaget these categories are sequenced in age as follows:

- Practice play (6 months to 2 years)
- Symbolic play (2 to 6 years)
- Games with rules (over 6 years).

As the child gets older his/her cognitive development is matched with increasingly sophisticated play activities or games where the child actively participates in his/her own learning. There is an assumption that the child's development of thought is sequenced and that each stage must be complete before moving on to the next.

At the practice play phase the young child is engaging in physical and exploratory play which Piaget suggests he/she must learn before moving to higher level play. In the play situation the child changes incoming information in order to understand this in his/her existing knowledge (assimilation). The child also changes in order to adapt to incoming information (accommodation). Play occurs when assimilation predominates over accommodation, this means that the child needs to develop certain skills, knowledge and experience before he/she can play. As he/she progresses from exploratory play and learns to pretend, the play activities become more symbolic. Finally, as he/she develops a sense of justice, the child learns to play games with rules. Consequently, the child distinguishes between play as repetition of an act already mastered and the repetition of an activity in order to understand it. Piaget viewed the adult as the provider of learning activities rather than an active participant in the child's learning.

Piaget's view of play has been criticised by many academics and practitioners including Brian Sutton-Smith (1966), who argues that he deals only with play behaviours and ignores the creative nature of play. Hutt (1966) suggests that when children overcome the exploratory phase of learning they can engage more effectively with play, thus separating exploration and play. Her 'Epistemic Play' refers to early exploratory play and 'Ludic Play' refers to the more sophisticated imaginative play. On the one hand during exploration the child was viewed as relatively serious and focused on asking 'What does this object do?' On the other hand, play behaviour was viewed as more varied and relaxed and as asking the question 'What can I do with this object?'

Singer and Singer (1990) highlight the importance of play in cognitive, physical and social development. Their research in recent decades is mainly on the subject of imaginative play. They refer to early childhood as the 'high season' for imaginative play. As children grow older, pretend play is less prevalent than other forms of play, such as games with rules, which are considered more socially acceptable. In contrast earlier theorists such as Hofstader (1979) claimed that pretend play never disappears from childhood through to adulthood and that we constantly create and change, providing a balance between fantasy and reality.

## Play as a form of expression

As discussed in the previous chapter, the child's sense of security is fundamental to play. When the child feels safe he/she can explore a range of emotions through play. Freud (1922) described all behaviour as motivated by the wishes of the individual. He viewed play as a process which enabled the child to feel in control and master of his/her own world. Erikson (1963) valued the play experience as a way of overcoming childhood disappointments and as a preparation for the practicalities of adult life. Similarly Bruce (1991) described play as a cathartic experience enabling the child to release anxiety and resolve future conflict. Winnicott (1990) stressed the value of transitional objects in the development of play. Across cultures, playthings such as clothing, teddies, etc., can act as a bridge between the child's dependency on his/her mother and gradual independence in his/her environment. These theorists emphasise the emotional experience of play. Their views can provide an explanation for why the child plays in a particular way and how emotional needs can be addressed through the medium of play.

## Play and education

The controversial role of play in educational settings has been the subject of ongoing discussion. This has been largely due to the lack of clarity about its educational value.

Friedrich Froebel (1906), the pioneer of the kindergarten and nursery school movement, saw play as a unifying force between the child, adult(s) and environment. He criticised rote-teaching and learning approaches and instead advocated play as making learning meaningful for children.

Isaacs (1929) viewed the role of play within the Early Years Curriculum as essential to the emotional and cognitive development of the child. Margaret McMillan (1860–1931) saw education as having a remediating function for the child. She considered play as having a significant place in education. She viewed play as a medium for skill development and experimentation thus emphasising the importance of indoor and outdoor play areas. In the UK, these ideas have been accepted as prerequisites for Early Years play provision.

According to Tina Bruce (1991), Froebel, Isaacs and McMillan saw play as central to the overall development of the child. She states that these pioneers of early education considered the child as a unit, with play as an integrating device. Maria Montessori's philosophy (1912) emphasised learning for real life through the fine-tuning of a child's cognitive skills. This was done through the provision of graded and structured tasks for the purpose of self-initiated learning with little scope for creativity. She viewed pretend and socio-dramatic play as primitive and escapist rather than promoting real learning for life. Since the Plowden Report (DES 1967) consolidated the view that childhood is important in itself and not simply a preparation for adulthood, early years curricula have recognised the significance of play in the education of young children.

## Play and chaology

The challenging concept of play can be explained in terms of Gleick's Chaos Theory (1988). This theory called Chaology is based on the idea that there is a non-linear relationship between the process and the product in all systems. Scientific measurement is often impossible due to the irregularity and uncertainty across a range of phenomenal principles. This theoretical framework fits neatly within an unstructured/undirected play situation. In the play environment the observer is never entirely sure what the child is bringing to the play situation or what he/she is getting out of it. This causes confusion and controversy regarding adults' understanding of play and the value they attach to it.

In Bruce's 'free flow play' (1991) approach she has adopted the principles of chaology. According to her, through play the child explores his/her environment in a random and complex way, testing his/her ideas, experimenting with his/her feelings and relationships while simultaneously developing skills and competence. The hallmark of free flow play is the opportunities provided in the play environment through available activities as opposed to adult direction.

## Interactionist views of play

Vygotsky (1978) saw play as a vehicle for social interaction rather than a dominant form of activity for young children. In his view, play provided an opportunity for the child to experience confidence and mastery. He emphasised the importance of pretend play for the development of the child's imagination and ideas for the future. Play can act as a facilitator for social interaction between the child's peers and adults helping him/her to make sense and create meaning from experience within a shared cultural framework. Vygotsky identifies a mediating role for the adult in the child's learning which can also be applied in the play context. Through play the child can move from his/her *actual* developmental level to his/her *potential* developmental level.

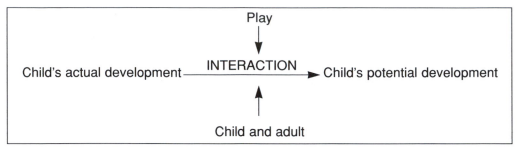

**Figure 2.2** Play and social interaction

Bandura's (1977) Social Learning Theory can be applied to a child's play. The imitation of adult and peer behaviour during play can lead to learning in the social context. Although it is accepted that not everything observed will be imitated, this depends on the child's disposition to learn including his/her experience, relationships with the model (adult/others) and his/her cognitive ability. Unlike Vygotsky, who viewed the learning potential of the child as dependent on interaction with others, Bandura considered the child's innate cognitive ability as directly related to learning in the social situation.

Smilansky (1990) emphasises the significance of pretend play for the cognitive development of the child. She believes that social skills are acquired through the child using his/her imagination, creativity and pretence. In the play situation the child not only plays with playthings and playmates but at a deeper level the child uses these interactions to play with ideas and meanings. In Klugman and Smilansky (1990) the distinction between the terms 'dramatic' and 'socio-dramatic play' is made.

When a child believes 'as if' he/she is somebody else then the child is involved in dramatic play. If the child interacts with at least one other child (or adult) while pretending, then their play is becoming socio-dramatic.

Like Vygotsky, Smilansky (1990) supports tutoring by adults and peers during pretend play. This can take the following forms:

• Modelling – joining in and showing the child how the role should be acted out.
• Verbal guidance – suggestions as to how the child should develop his/her role.
• Thematic fantasy training – using a familiar story as a basis for exploring themes.
• Imaginative play training – make-believe activities where the focus is on fantasy rather than role-playing.

She found that play-tutoring supported:

• the amount and complexity of fantasy and socio-dramatic play;
• the development of the child's social, cognitive and language skills.

The main focus of Smilansky's approach to developing pretend play skills is the extent to which the play experience is directed for the child. The child is guided by modelling and teaching specific play skills by the tutor, in the expert role, as opposed to through skilled questioning and the teaching of principles.

Haste (1987) takes a social constructivist view of play. Like Vygotsky he indicates the importance of culture and context on children's play. On the one hand the child's play reflects popular culture, but on the other hand the child's understanding of the world is developed through play, thus making the process one of constant change and development.

He points out that play produces change at three levels:

- Intra-individual: within-child cognitive changes as a result of the child's play experiences.
- Interpersonal: meanings and conventions are learned from relationships with others.
- Social-cultural: learning takes place within the wider socio-cultural context.

In addition to the sense of power that play gives to children enabling them to move between activities in a range of contexts, it also presents challenges to support the child's development.


## Play as a process

In the previous discussion around definitions (Chapter 1) the notion of play as product-led or process-led was discussed. Bruner (1972) emphasised the importance of language and structure in the learning environment. He was interested in looking at play as process-led rather than task-oriented and described play as an approach to action not a kind of activity. In 1991 he outlined a role for play as a vehicle for learning about society's rules and conventions.

Janet Moyles (1988) also supports this process-led view. As a contemporary play theorist, she describes play as either free or directed, where the function of free play is to enable exploration and the function of directed play is to develop mastery. These processes do not occur in isolation but they may happen in sequence or simultaneously.

The authors have an interactionist view of play where the child and the environment are interconnected. Play does not occur in a vacuum. The child's individuality and the specific components of the context enable play to occur. Figure 2.3 depicts the authors' conceptual framework for play.

This view of play as an interlinking, everchanging phenomenon with both process and product has a socio-constructivist flavour. The child as an individual brings to the play situation his/her strengths and weaknesses in terms of his/her skills, knowledge and experience. Children's ability, maturity and physical development are particularly relevant to play. Equally the play materials,

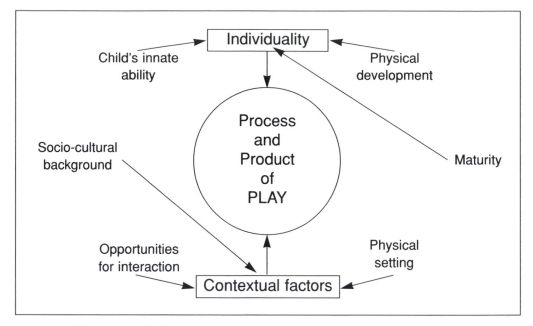

**Figure 2.3** An interactionist model of play

activities made available to the child, the socio-cultural backdrop and his/her opportunities for interaction with others. The emotional development of the child can be influenced by changing relationships during the play process. Where one or more factors are deficient there may be a need to compensate through emphasis on other factors, e.g. where a child may have difficulties with learning there may be a need for increased adult involvement in play. The combination of within-child and contextual factors all affect how the child plays and the outcome of play.

## Chapter 3

# Play – culture-free or culture-biased?

Bob Hughes (1990) described the play process as that which brings us into the contact with the environment and the culture around us. He describes childhood as a journey through an unknown and unfamiliar place where the child is in the role of a visitor and play is his/her means of discovery, forging a relationship between the child and his/her environment. Before we talk about culture we need to be clear about what we mean by the concept. Culture is as difficult to define as play. This is likely to be due to the intangible nature of the elements of culture. Every individual's thoughts, beliefs, hopes and aspirations are representative of their culture, consequently an individual cannot be separated from his/her culture. According to Howitt and Owusu-Bempeh (1999 p. 20), 'One's cultural background is inseparable from one's psychological process.'

Sociologists and anthropologists explain the concept of culture in a variety of ways. In its general sense it embraces all of that which is symbolic: 'the learned, ideational aspects of human society' (Jenks 1993 pp. 1–12). He summarises the various meanings of the concept of culture in four categories:

1. An *intellectual* category: 'culture becomes intelligible as a general state of mind. It carries with it the idea of perfection, a goal or an aspiration of individual human achievement or emancipation.'
2. A more *personified and consolidated* category: 'culture invokes a state of intellectual and/or moral development in society. This is a position linking culture with the idea of civilization and one that is informed by the evolutionary theories of Charles Darwin (1809-82).'
3. An *expressive and definite* category: 'culture viewed as the collected body of arts and intellectual work within one society: that is very much an everyday language of the term "culture" and carries along with it senses of particularity, exclusivity, elitism, specialist knowledge and training and socialization.'
4. A *social* category: 'culture regarded as the whole way of life of a people: this is the pluralist and potentially democratic sense of the concept that has come to be the zone of concern within sociology and anthropology and latterly, within a more localized sense, cultural studies.'

The authors define culture in accordance with Jenks' social category, 'a way of life, which binds the thoughts, beliefs, and language of a group in a specific context' (Sayeed and Guerin 1997 p. 53). It is passed from generation to generation and often changes over time. In traditional cultures changes occur at a slower rate than non-traditional cultures, often for socio-economic, demographic and geographical reasons. This slow pace of change should not devalue traditional cultures as supported by Montague 1997 p. 21 (in Howitt and Owusu-Bempah) when he said 'No culture is superior to that of another'. This view needs to be well understood and recognised by those who have mindsets about superior and inferior cultures.

Winnicott (1990) offers a creative definition of culture as 'located in potential space between the human being and the environment' (Sayeed and Guerin 1997 p. 55). Life's experiences are determined by the use of this space, which is infiltrated by culture. Whiting and Whiting (1975) view play and culture as a two-way process. In their opinion play is affected by cultural influences and acts as an expression of culture. According to Bruner (1996) culture helps us to organise and understand our worlds in a way that is easily communicated. If we accept that play is a voluntary, spontaneous and enjoyable experience then Walker's definition of culture identifies a clear link between play and culture. According to him, culture provides the medium in which 'one should thrive, the body and spirit simultaneously' (Walker 1997 p. 50).

Common cultural factors define groups but also separate them from other groups, hence the concept of cultural identity. Culture guides and regulates how the person lives his/her life from the 'cradle to the grave'. From the authors' standpoint, the process and product of play are a direct result of the interaction between the individual child and his/her environment. If one accepts that play is the dominant form of activity for a young child this cannot be separated from the context in which it takes place.

In every culture learning begins with the child's family. Whiting and Edwards (1988) refer to this as primary socialisation. This socialisation process transmits an individualistic or collective view of life, depending on the attributions of a particular culture. In Western cultures (e.g. UK and USA) considerable emphasis is placed on looking out for oneself or meeting one's own needs. This attitude and approach to life is advantageous in terms of self-realisation and progress but can obstruct collaboration and co-existence. In contrast, traditional cultures (e.g. some Asian and African societies) promote collectivism where importance is attached to group allegiance. This cultural characteristic has implications for children's style and pattern of learning and playing. Research by Allen (1997) showed that children from traditional cultures perform better on group rather than individual tasks. Even when second generation children from a collectivist background are living in an individualistic society, research has shown that their learning and behaviour is characterised by group loyalties.

## Challenges to play and culture

Roopnarine *et al.* (1998) found that there are not many detailed studies of children's play in different cultural settings. Participants have mainly been from North American and European families and children, consequently the findings may be biased and limited in their generalisability across cultures, gender, social class and ethnicity (Rubin *et al.* 1983; Johnson *et al.* 1987 and Hughes 1994). In the authors' view the information available should be subject to critical analysis before conclusions are drawn that may lead to stereotyping. Howitt and Owusu-Bempah (1999) emphasised inaccurate professional knowledge sources which were based on proactive information gathering rather than statistically significant research. Negative beliefs and assumptions corrupt professional knowledge further. This can lead to stereotypes and negative portrayals of children from specific cultural groups with damaging consequences for their play and learning.

There exists a combination of evidence and assumptions about the differences and similarities between the play of children of industrialised and non-industrialised societies. Authors such as Feitelson (1977) have been criticised for the suggestions that traditional cultures, which are based on stable beliefs, attitudes and expectations, have a negative effect on the child's imaginative play. In economically secure societies where early years education can afford to include play, it is assumed that greater value is attached to play. In societies with unstable economies, play provision is less formal and there may be an assumption that play is considered less valuable.

As discussed in the previous chapters the published literature on the subject of play fails to provide a single comprehensive theory of play which incorporates its diverse nature. However, theorists such as Bruner (1972), Vygotsky (1978) and others have given socio-cultural explanations for child development which further an understanding of the relationship between culture and play.

## Parental influences on children's play

Through the process of socialisation children acquire the standards, values and knowledge of their culture. This process starts as soon as the child is born, thus parents play a pivotal role. It is generally accepted that parental involvement affects the quality and process of play. Fiese (1990) found that children's play lasted longer and was more sophisticated when they played with their mothers than when they played by themselves. Other researchers found that parents adjusted their level of play to that of their children to maximise its attractiveness.

While children are playing they are socialising, and during playful interactions with their parents they learn and absorb aspects of their culture. Roopnarine *et al.* (1998) reviewed the literature and summarised cross-cultural views about child development and child-rearing practices relating to play. The following themes emerged when traditional and non-traditional cultures were compared and contrasted:

• Children's play is more likely to reflect rituals and customs in traditional societies.
• One-to-one play is more prevalent in non-traditional societies.
• In traditional cultures play tends to occur more often in work-related settings.
• Group participation, interdependence and community values are transmitted through play in traditional cultures whereas self-reliance, independence and competition are encouraged by non-traditional cultures.
• Gender differentiation has been observed in the parent–child play in non-traditional cultures but this has not been consistently observed in other societies.
• Variations of games such as peek-a-boo and pat-a-cake played between parents and their children can occur across traditional and non-traditional cultures.

Parental involvement in their children's play may run along a continuum. At one extreme is the parent who is not aware of their child's play and any role they may have within it. At the other end of the continuum is the parent who may intentionally exclude themselves from their child's play as they are conscious of being interfering and invasive. Within any culture these extremes can exist but a parent's/carer's clear understanding of his/her role and a reasonable level of involvement can enrich the child's play in any given context.

## Gender differences in children's play

Due to the complexity of making cultural comparisons around children's play, research has often focused on gender differences. Observers of children's play regularly comment on how young boys and girls play differently and often separately. Why does this happen?

Anecdotal observations by the authors in inner London schools reveal separate play patterns between boys and girls. Boys tend to re-enact fantasy situations such as fighting a war, cops and robbers, etc., whereas girls tend to act out real situations from their immediate culture, e.g. feeding a doll in the role of a mother. It is debatable as to whether the gender preferences for particular types of play are the result of socialisation processes where expectations around what boys and girls play and how they play are learned.

The literature would suggest that considerable research has been conducted on gender comparisons.

Heino *et al.* (1994) described the dimorphic nature of children's play behaviour across age ranges. Surprisingly, age, socio-economic levels, race or ethnicity seemed to have little effect in contrast with gender.

Neppyl and Murray (1997) reviewed the literature in relation to pre-schoolers. Their paper focused on sex-stereotypical behaviour under the following headings:

- Selection of same sex playmates: As early as 1933, Parten found that during free play pre-school children elected to play with same-sex playmates. Jacklin and Maccoby (1978) showed increased interaction when children were paired with same sex peers. The authors' observations of pre-school children's preferences for same-sex playmates support this finding. This is exemplified in Figures 3.1 and 3.2 where children were engaged in water play in an inner London nursery school.
- Social dominance: Serbin *et al.* (1982) found that girls used polite requests and persuasion to get what they wanted in the play situation, whereas boys relied on commands and physical force.
- Gender preferences for sex-typed toys: Martin and Little (1990) showed that young children had developed an understanding of gender as a social category, which accounted for their choice of toys.
- Gender differences in terms of play patterns: Neppyl and Murray (1997) found that interactive, imaginative play tended to occur most where children were grouped in same-sex pairs. This is largely because they opted for different kinds of play activities in relation to their gender.

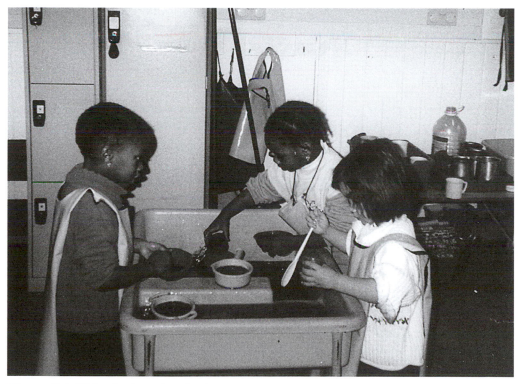

**Figure 3.1** Girls playing at water tray

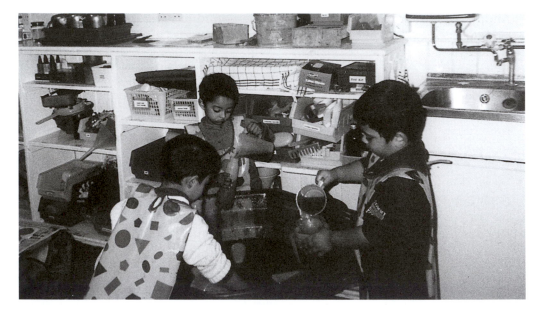

**Figure 3.2** Boys playing at water tray

Thorne (1993) described how boys play differently to girls when together. The main differences were as follows:

- Boys played in larger groups than girls.
- Boys engaged in loud public games whereas girls had a preference for quiet, private games.
- Boys' play was hierarchical in nature whereas girls' games were collaborative.

A small study was conducted by the authors in the inner London Education Authority of Tower Hamlets (1995) where the largest ethnic groups are Bangladeshi and White-English. Interviews across some early years education settings revealed that, on the one hand, teachers did not observe significant differences between the play of children from different cultures but on the other hand the gender difference was easily identified.

According to a cross-cultural study by Lindsey *et al.* (1997) parents may contribute to children's gender-specific styles of play. They influence their children's play by modelling some play behaviours and treating and rewarding their sons and daughters differently. Some examples of the findings of Lindsey and his colleagues include:

- Boys were more likely to play physically.
- Girls were more likely to engage in pretend play.
- The mother's presence seemed to encourage pretend play for both boys and girls.
- Fathers of boys were more inclined to engage in physical play than mothers or fathers of girls.

The authors conducted a study of Parental Perspectives on Play in Tower Hamlets (1999). When interviewed, most parents said that their lifestyle (work schedules, working habits, family composition, etc.) impacted on their children's play more than ethnicity, language and religion. The concept of a mother staying at home, playing and caring for her child is no longer a viable option for many modern working parents. When parents are working there is an onus on them to ensure that their children can avail themselves of appropriate play opportunities in the community. Consequently resources at the local community level affect the quality of children's play at an individual level and this may be a more significant factor in children's play than the influence of culture.

## The play/work link across cultures

In the UK, young children's play is often described as their 'work' and vice versa. The following parent – child conversation is typical at the end of a day spent in an early years setting:

> *Mother: Did you have a good day at the nursery?*
> *Child:    Yeah.*
> *Mother: What did you do?*
> *Child:    Played.*
> *Mother: I know you played in the morning ... what did you do after dinner?*
> *Child:    I played the measuring game with Sheila (teacher) and John (peer).*
> *Mother: Did you do any work?*
> *Child looks at mother with surprised facial expression.*
> *Child:    I'll play with Sheila again tomorrow ... It was a nice game, Mum.*
>  *(With excited tone of voice)*

The boundaries between work and play become more obvious as children get older and their time becomes increasingly subject to adult direction and product-led activities. The transition from early years provision to school is often a difficult time for young children due to the shift away from play-based activities to an academic curriculum. The introduction of 'play-time' to the school day infers that time in the classroom is no longer for playing and children quickly start to differentiate between what is play and what is not play.

Roopnarine *et al.* (1998) outlined the dimensions of work and play by using two categories:

• Directed activities: mostly work.
• Undirected social activities: mainly play.

In traditional cultures children are often involved in adults' work, e.g. fishing, herding or selling. When they are not being directed by adults, they create opportunities to engage in activities of their own choosing, i.e. play. The fluid movement between play and work often includes re-enactments of scenes from work activities, making a distinction between work and play difficult from an observer's perspective. Children from communities such as the Kenyan Gikuyan or Nigerian Igan have been found to mimic adult roles in preparation for adult life (Bloch and Adler 1994).

It is known that when children from poorer socio-economic settings need to work to supplement the family income there is less time and fewer materials available. In the UK, until as recently as 1833, children were commonly working up to 12 hours per day in mines, factories or shops. The Factories Enquiries Committee recommended a reduction in working hours by 12 per cent which could be replaced by religious and moral education. Children working to earn money is a greater reflection of economic conditions rather than the cultural status of the society. Material poverty *per se* does not prevent children from playing. In a stimulating environment the child will develop a sense of playfulness and he/she will invent his/her play from simple materials from nature or rejects from adults (Bloch and Pelligrini 1989). An interesting study by Whiting and Edwards (1988) looked at the play opportunities within and outside the home. They found that the greater the distance from the child's home the more play opportunities were available to children in post-industrialised societies. Boys were found to be more likely to play in streets and parks whereas girls often played in/near the home. Hence boys had more opportunities to develop leadership qualities, personal and social skills through play. As a result of an increased focus on formal education and curriculum in recent years the distinction between work and play, which was previously unclear in some cultures, has become clearer.

## Play, culture and early years provision

In societies where play opportunities are formally available to young children in settings such as nurseries, early years units and playgroups, the educational enrichment value of play has been recognised. In the UK successive governments have struggled to recommend how play could be used as a medium for early learning. Recent references to 'structured play' provision in early years settings infer the active involvement of adults who are knowledgeable and skilled in meeting the developmental and learning needs of young children. According to the *Early Learning Goals* (DfEE 1999) during the foundation stage adults are expected to interact with children through play and structure play activities appropriately.

Society's view of the importance of play varies considerably. In countries such as China and Japan, where formal educational approaches were practised, recognition has been given to the role of childhood play. With the advancement of technology the types of play children engaged in previously have been eroded. Traditional outdoor games such as bows and arrows, flying kites, etc., have been substituted with indoor video games and other manufactured toys (Takeuchi 1994). This phenomenon is becoming a cause for concern in all modern societies where children are interacting less often with nature and more frequently with machines.

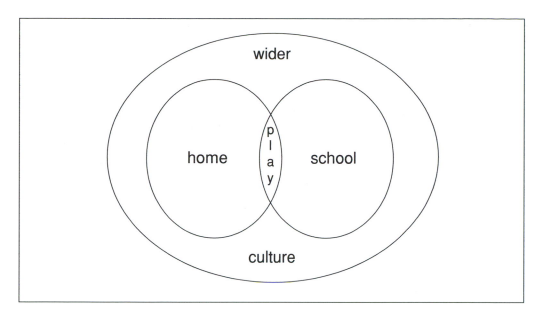

**Figure 3.3** Influences on play

The multimedia and marketing culture of the new millenium has influenced what children play with rather than how they play. Consequently, parents and educators are important providers of natural play experiences and assessors of play skills. Technological advancement poses challenges for parents and teachers who want to provide a healthy balance between natural and man-made learning experiences so that the child can achieve his/her developmental and learning potential. Research has shown that over-indulgence in 'screen-focused' activities may enhance some areas of the child's functioning but it has its drawbacks. Griffiths (1998) found evidence of addiction to fruit machines under certain conditions amongst children and adolescents, the effects of which include: school truancy, poor academic performance, criminal behaviour and aggressive behaviour.

Every child has an immediate and wider culture. Although his/her home is the immediate culture where the child's early care, socialisation and learning occur, the influence of cultures beyond his/her home and the wider world gradually increase and shape a view of the world through his play. When he/she moves to an educational setting this new culture is simultaneously accommodated and diversified.

Play providers need to reflect the culture of the community in order to enhance the play of local children. The school's ethos and the cultural experience of the teacher can either have a positive or negative effect on the cultural appropriateness of the play provision. In some cultures, religious customs and celebrations feature in children's play and should be appreciated and understood by the play providers. Cultural learning styles (e.g. holistic *vs* analytical) must also be taken into account by educators when play is central to what they are providing for children in the early years.

Farver *et al.* (1995) in a comparative study of Korean-American and Anglo-American pre-schoolers suggest the influence of the teacher's culture on the style of play provision. This study showed that while the teacher can provide adequate materials, extended periods of time and space for playing, his/her attitude towards play is equally significant. Where a teacher's cultural background does not promote play as a medium for learning then the teacher's own attempts to use play to facilitate learning are less likely to be successful. This study also stresses that a teacher's cultural background supersedes his/her professional training. Thus where a teacher's cultural background emphasises the value of play then any training contrary to this will have minimum effect on his/her practice. Early years educators need to scrutinise their own cultural values and beliefs as well as those of the children they are providing for, so that they can make conscious and informed decisions about the objectives of play.

If early years play is a source of learning then play should also be a medium for assessment. Each time a child's play is assessed, the participants, i.e. the adult and the child, bring the elements of their own culture to bear on the situation. Therefore play-based assessment cannot be considered free of cultural influence. This highlights the difficulties in the identification of cultural factors influencing learning. If a cultural difference exists between the assessor and the player, it is the assessor's responsibility to gain a sound knowledge of the child's background and experience, making the assessment process and the outcome more meaningful.

Where partnerships between home and school exist, teachers will want to respond to parental expectations of what constitutes early years education. Swedener and John (1989) found that when parents have a positive attitude to play their children are likely to be involved in a high level of imaginative and creative play. Curtis (1994) suggests that modern parents in small families need to be involved in playing with their children in order to teach their children how to play with their peers in the absence of siblings.

## The status of play

The status of play around the world is constantly changing. In his extensive study, Benjamin Bloom (1964) found that 80 per cent of all learning at eighteen years was attained through play by eight years of age. He also found that 50 per cent was attained by four years through play. In the UK, pre-Plowden education trends in the 1960s and 1970s in England and Wales allowed for greater creativity in the classroom where play was often used as a learning medium. At a local level, voluntary bodies such as Toy Libraries and Play Associations managed to sustain some adult interest in play provision in schools and the community. While the ethos and cultural influence of school and family systems can influence the child's play, resource implications have become a pertinent issue.

At an international level the child's right to play has been recognised and emphasised by the International Association of the Right of the Child to Play during conferences in Stockholm in 1987 and subsequently in Tokyo in 1990. The IPA aims to support worldwide policy development for play provision. Although the recognition of a child's right to play has been established in many countries, the concept of early years play as an educational tool has not been adopted internationally.

Article 31 of the UN Convention on the Rights of the Child advocates the child's right to rest, leisure, play and recreational activities and participation in cultural and artistic life. The importance of play irrespective of culture and socio-economic status is emphasised. Hodgkin and Newell (1998) in the Implementation Handbook summarise the main principles, referring to play as 'a forgotten right as it appears to the adults as a luxury activity rather than a necessity to life' (p. 417). Interestingly it is proposed that play is exclusively an activity of children without the control of adults or constraints of rules. This implies that play is not a component of schooling and play-type activities in school are described as 'recreational' rather than play. Many countries have embraced the principles of Article 31 but putting these into practice has significant implications, firstly for changes in adult attitudes in society, secondly, resources and thirdly, cooperation of different levels of government and agencies. The status of play can only be enhanced if Article 31 is given legislative status at a national level.

International organisations such as UNICEF, UNESCO and UNHCR as well as Non-Governmental Organisations such as Oxfam and Save The Children who work for children's welfare need to be vigilant in promoting the rights of all children, including the right of children to play. Various cultural modes and the spontaneity of an individual child's play should be considered as assets in the play context. Similarly the child's ability, race, colour and place of birth should never be viewed as barriers to play.

*Chapter 4*

# Play and emotions: raising awareness of the relationship between children's play and emotional development

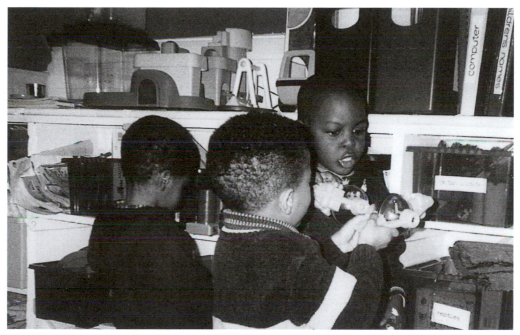

**Figure 4.1** A group of children emotionally absorbed in play

Most parents and adults in the caring professions such as teachers, psychologists and social workers are aware that when children play they are involved in an emotional activity. Emotions can best be described as feelings elicited by interactions. Cole and Cole (1996) support this view by defining emotions as feelings aroused by experiences. For the purposes of this chapter the terms emotions and feelings will be used interchangeably. In the literature and general discourse there is a tendency to confuse emotion and behaviour. The former is a state rather than an expression. To give an example, sadness is an emotion whereas crying is an observable behaviour, which can indicate sadness.

The child's early emotional development is inextricably linked with his/her opportunities for socialisation. As the baby explores the environment he/she uses the mother as a secure base (Bowlby 1973). This 'attachment relationship' is usually the first opportunity for the child to experience the world beyond him/herself thus the sensitive response of the mother/caregiver is fundamental for bonding to occur.

Ainsworth *et al.* (1978) examined the relationship between early attachment and the child's later emotional and cognitive development. A secure attachment to mother/carer in early childhood allows the child to develop an 'internal working model'. This has implications for the child's other relationships beyond the mother/carer.

> The internal working model of relationships reflects earlier experiences. The quality of these influences children's sense of self and also expectations of how they can form relationships with others.
>
> (Morley-Williams *et al.* 1995 p. 48)

In the 1970s Bowlby's attachment theory was used to develop the concept of Nurture Grouping in the Inner London Education Authority (Boxall 1976). Its purpose was to support young children with 'attachment disorders' at school. For children to be included in Nurture Groups their presenting behaviours would include:

- disruptive, acting out and tantrum behaviour
- severely withdrawn behaviour
- poor global communication
- very limited social skills.

In the cases of these children, their behaviours and underlying feelings will have significantly affected their educational performance. Nurture Groups as an intervention are discussed in more detail later in this chapter.

Emotional development is 'within child' but the process through which emotional changes take place is dependent on the child's opportunities for social experiences (interaction) and learning potential. Taking an interactionist perspective, a child's emotions at a given time seem to link his/her past experiences with future expectations as presented in Figure 4.2.

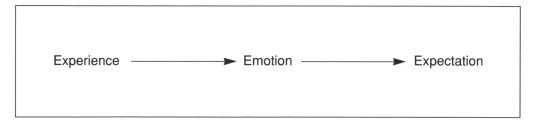

**Figure 4.2** How emotions develop

For adults who want to understand a child's emotional needs and provide play it is essential to explore the child's previous experiences, find out how he/she feels about current events in his/her life and elicit what his/her expectations for the future are.

## Thoughts, emotions and empathy

As children grow they become aware of their own emotions and also learn to share the feelings and emotions of others (develop empathy). According to Hoffman (1991) children can feel empathy at an early age but as they get older their empathy broadens and they learn to interpret and respond appropriately to the behaviour of others. There is a close link between a child's cognitive and emotional development. A child's emotions affect the way he/she thinks and acts and his/her thoughts affect the emotions he/she experiences. Hoffman's theory of empathy is linked closely with Piaget's theory of cognitive development. It is based on the principle that as children get older their thinking becomes more sophisticated and their ability to empathise becomes refined as they understand themselves better in relation to others. If this is the case, by mid-childhood the child should be able to:

- understand his/her own emotions
- empathise with the emotions of others
- regulate his/her feelings and expressions.

However, a study by Bishof-Kohler (cited in Perner 1991) showed a significant relationship between a child's level of self-recognition and empathetic behaviour. This was irrespective of the age of the child and would suggest that the age of the development of empathy is variable.

Normally in early childhood a child's sense of self as distinct from others develops in the context of the family, the peer group and the wider community. This sense of self is used as a reference point for understanding the emotions of others and the two are inextricably linked. The child's development of awareness of others' mental states, beliefs and desires is called a Theory of Mind. Pervasive developmental disorders such as childhood autism are characterised by severe social and communication impairments and have been linked with a deficient Theory of Mind. Leslie and Frith (1990) hypothesised about how children with autism lack a Theory of Mind, which prevents them from understanding the emotions of others and responding appropriately. This may explain why children with autism display behaviours such as poor eye contact, ignoring others, absorption in their own world and resistance to change. These behaviours have implications for how these children play, what they play with and how the play providers meet their needs.

## Link between play and emotion

Play provides a medium for interaction allowing the child to express and explore his/her emotions. The authors' definition of play alludes to its emotional features: 'play assumes absorption, concentration and an escape to a world' (Sayeed and Guerin 1997 p. 46). This definition highlights the unobservable emotional components of play which occur in addition to observable behaviours. When a child is deeply absorbed in play it is similar to a hypnotic or relaxed state. Through play the child can experiment with *pretend* and *real* emotions. The following extract depicts an actual scene observed in a nursery school playground where real and pretend emotions overlapped.

*A group of three boys and two girls were playing a game of 'Cops and Robbers'. Some were on the scooters and tricycles and others were running frantically between the grassy areas and concrete. As the game progressed, shouting, screaming, laughter and large hand gestures were observed as expressions of their emotions and indications of their levels of absorption and pretence.*

✳ ✳ ✳

*In the midst of their game a boy on a tricycle drove into the game area and without looking ahead collided with one of the other boys who was running while pretending to be a robber. The 'robber' fell over and grazed his knee badly; suddenly the game became real. He started to cry aloud, one of his playmates ran to the teacher for help looking quite distressed. Another child showed anger by shouting at the 'culprit' on the tricycle. At the sight of the blood on her friend's knee a third playmate covered her eyes as if she needed to protect herself from this painful sight.*

As adults our most vivid memories of childhood play are often associated with extreme feelings rather than specific events. In her book *Play Is A Feeling*, Brenda Crowe (1983) recalls and interprets the feelings of childhood (hers and others) from the memories of intense sensory experiences. She interviewed many parents of young children who remembered play vividly, including the look, sound, touch, smell and taste of things and their child's positive feelings such as joy and negative feelings such as distress. In her work she explored the creative and healing nature of play and how adults can use play to cope with change and relieve stress.

In the context of play previous memories can elicit current emotions in the child, which form expectations for the future (see Figure 4.2). This fits with Piaget's view that play moulds reality to fit the child's own thinking. Where a child is feeling emotionally secure he/she is able to use his/her past experience and innate ability more effectively to accommodate incoming information through play. Therefore there is an inextricable link between the child's social, emotional and cognitive development.

In the following play sequence the children are learning and enhancing their ability to pretend. There is evidence of sharing, negotiation and an awareness of each other's feelings. The absorption and concentration of the players allowed two play themes to run side by side.

*Rahima, Alice and Ola are playing with the washing machine in the home corner in a nursery.*
*Ola:*     *Look I'm washing the baby's clothes.*
*Rahima: I'm Mum . . . I do it.*
*Alice:*    *Give me the clothes . . . I'm Mum (starts to cry).*
*Ola gives the clothes to Alice.*
*Ola:*     *I'll do the washing powder.*
*Rahima moves away and starts to feed the dolly, ignoring the others.*
*Ola:*     *I'm the Dad.*
*Alice:*    *Let me push (gesturing to the buttons on the washing machine).*
*Both Alice and Ola put the clothes in the washing machine while Rahima is absorbed in her own play with the doll.*

## Playfulness

A child needs to feel emotionally secure before he/she can develop a playful disposition. He/she should be able to imagine, share a sense of humour, be open and communicative, be flexible and persevere as he/she seeks out new experiences. For example in his/her pretend play a child should be able to move quickly and easily from one role to another without feeling self-conscious or in fear of criticism. When a child is playful, he/she is creative and imaginative. Playfulness ensures that play is a self-motivating and enjoyable process leading to learning. According to Sinetar (1991) playfulness encourages experimentation, de-emphasises the need to be perfect and builds self-esteem. Trumbell (in Goldhaber 1994, p. 3) compares the child's playfulness with the experimentation of a scientist. 'The playfulness of the scientist, like the playfulness of the child, is intense, but permits the freedom to explore and to try out a wide range of ideas with no fear of being wrong'. Playful children are curious, ask questions, take time to explore play materials in order to understand, use prediction to form, test and reject their ideas. Throughout this process the playful child will enjoy the play experience while communicating with peers and others.

The following extract depicts the imagination, excitement and emotion of a child's play experience with clear evidence of his playful disposition while carrying a book on his head:

I had a book on top of my head. I had to get up the stairs without it falling off. If it fell off I would die. It was a hardback book, heavy, the best kind for carrying on your head. I couldn't remember which one it was. I knew all the books in the house. I know their shapes and smells. I knew what pages would be open if I held them with the spine on the ground and let the sides drop. I knew all the books but couldn't remember the one on my head. I'd find out when I got to the top, touched my bedroom door and got back down again. Then I could take it off my head – I'd bring my head forward slowly and let it slide off and I'd catch it – and see what it was. I could have seen the corner of the cover if I'd looked up very carefully; I could have got the same from the colour of the corner. But it was too dangerous. I had a mission to complete. Steady was better than too slow I'd go all unsteady and I'd think I'd never make it and the book would fall off. Death.'     (Doyle 1994 p. 75)

Valett (1983) developed a theory to explain how children progress from being playful to being imaginative in their learning, extending this concept to adulthood. He outlined five phases including:

- *sensory exploration* (0–5 years approx.): the child eagerly explores the environment using his senses;
- *egocentric speculation* (2–7 years approx.): the child imagines, fantasises and attributes life-like qualities to inert objects;
- *personal experimentation* (6–10 years approx.): the child experiments with what he can see and hear using a trial and error approach;
- *symbolic representation* (11–15 years approx.): the young adolescent represents his/her imaginative experiences in symbolic form such as drawing, dancing and painting;
- *functional verification* (23–onwards): as a result of his/her experiences the young adult becomes more creative and productive, making changes to himself and others.

According to Valett, an adult can support the development of playfulness in children through opportunities for play within this framework.


## Stages of play and the emotional development of the child

The play process provides an integrating mechanism for all aspects of a child's development. Play usually develops in broad stages depending on the child's individuality and opportunities for interaction with his/her environment. As he/she gets older his/her play moves from simple, exploratory activities to more abstract games. During this process the child's interactions become more complex with implications for his/her emotional development. The authors propose that the child's emotional development evolves from play to meet basic needs to more independent and social play, where context acts as a catalyst. This is summarised in Table 4.1.

At an early stage of a child's life and through exploration of the immediate environment, a child's emotional development begins. Izard (1978) claims that

**Table 4.1** Stages of play from an interactionist perspective

| Stage | Play activity | Context |
|---|---|---|
| 1 | Exploring | Self and caregiver(s) |
| 2 | Manipulating | Self, caregiver(s) and object |
| 3 | Imagining | Self, others and objects |
| 4 | Game playing | Self, others, objects and structures |

infants are born with innate emotions whereas Barrett and Campos (1987) conceptualise emotion as 'a system of processes that govern the functional relationship between infant and environment' (Bremner 1995).

In time, the child manipulates his/her environment more purposefully and develops emotional responses, e.g. he/she develops an awareness of danger in order to safeguard his/her own well being. He/she engages with objects as well as people and derives different responses evoking various emotions such as anger and sadness.

As the child grows he/she develops higher-level thinking skills such as pretending, imagining and representing. His/her play allows him/her to express his/her feelings in response to his interaction with others and objects (toys). He/she develops higher level emotions such as shame, guilt and pride.

A child's involvement in game playing incorporates feelings and behaviours in response to social rules. The structures and rules around play provide opportunities and constraints for the development of appropriate emotional responses and behaviours. Social expectations around sharing, negotiation and conformity need to evolve for play to progress. If the child's emotional maturity does not allow him/her to engage with the structure, rules and context for games then the play disintegrates. According to Winnicott (1971) successful interactions between children depend on their mutual awareness of whether they are playing or not. For play to thrive the player needs to be totally aware and involved in order to understand the play activity and find a role within it.

## How does play reflect emotions?

As an observer, one can only assume a child's emotional state on the basis of his/her behaviour during play. While there is a temptation for adults to over-interpret children's emotions during play, adults who participate in children's play by sharing their agenda over time are more likely to understand and interpret the emotions of the child. Quite often emotional states need to be identified from behavioural responses, as young children are less likely to express how they feel using words. All emotions can be found along a continuum, e.g. a child could be very angry, moderately angry or slightly angry. When a child is in a relaxed emotional state during play, his/her behavioural responses could include occupying him/herself, smiling or laughing. This positive emotional state can have the following benefits for the child:

- supports his/her positive interactions with others
- helps him/her to create his/her own world
- teaches him/her to avoid interruption
- allows him/her to set his/her own agenda
- motivates him/herself intrinsically
- expresses his/her happiness

Likewise if a child is feeling excited he/she could respond by screaming, laughing or shouting. The benefits of play for the child could include:

- support for his/her interactions with others
- expenditure of physical energy
- extended physical or verbal self-expression
- eliciting of reactions (positive or negative) from his/her environment
- increased interaction with his/her environment
- moulding of his/her and others' behaviour

## Others' views of the emotional benefits of play

The emotional benefits of play have been acknowledged by academics in the field of child development and by professionals who work with children. Freud (1922) viewed childhood play as a way of overcoming childhood anxieties and frustrations encountered during real-life interactions with others. Opportunities to re-enact adult situations during role-play allow the child to avoid childhood restrictions in order to create and manage his/her own world. Through play he makes his/her environment safer and less stressful, e.g. a role-play of a visit to the doctor's surgery allows a child to test feelings about having an injection. Susan Isaacs (1929) based at the Institute of Education in London viewed play as beneficial to the child's overall development but especially his/her emotional and cognitive development. According to her, 'play is indeed the child's work and the means whereby he grows and develops. Active play can be looked upon as sign of mental health; and its absence, either of some inborn defect or of mental illness' (Isaacs 1929, quoted in Smith and Cowie 1991 p. 82). Although this view could be considered extreme, the necessity for children to play to express their emotions is widely accepted.

Erikson (1963), a student of Freud, valued the play experience in the third of his eight stages of child development. He viewed play as a way of overcoming childhood disappointments and as a preparation for the practicalities of adult life.

Unlike Freud, he took into account the cultural setting for the child's play and emphasised the importance of social interaction for emotional development. Winnicott (1971) identified a play object/toy or 'transitional object' as a stepping stone initially between the child and his/her mother/carer and ultimately towards independence in the wider social context. Thus the child learns to cope with separation anxieties and develops emotional maturity. The adult's understanding of the significance of a transitional object is essential to support this process.

Play allows passive emotions to become active experiences. Play can also help the child to gather and organise his/her emotional experiences. As a medium, it is actively used by skilled childcare professionals to understand children's needs in order to provide suitable help. In play therapy, children are assisted by a therapist to express their frustrations and feelings while discovering what they can do and who they are. New understandings emerge through play as the process of acting on materials, objects, sounds, space and time becomes more meaningful. In a structured play setting, feelings of inadequacy, helplessness and rejection are overcome through the therapist's warmth and sensitivity. According to Ablon (1996) in the context of play therapy, play enables the child to communicate at two levels, within him/herself and with the therapist. Specific play therapy techniques address the child's hidden aggression and sexual impulses. Feelings that are troublesome and important can be dealt with and resolved, thus play has a cathartic, remediating benefit.

With adaptation, play therapy can be used to meet the emotional needs of children with special educational needs. Amongst this group of children feelings of inadequacy, helplessness and rejection are common because they are unable, or are perceived to be unable, to engage in all activities in the same way as their peers. Carmichael (1994) advocates person-centred play therapy for children with physical disabilities. This is based on free play where the therapist provides empathy, warmth and respect for the child through observing, encouraging and reflecting the child's feelings. The nature and outcome of therapy is dependent on the severity of child's special educational needs and the flexibility and creativity of the therapist.

Play therapy can be offered to groups of children as well as individuals. The Nurture Group concept (Boxall 1976) has recently resurged in the UK with the support of educational psychologists and other professionals. These groups take the form of small discrete classes in inclusive school settings with a high level of adult support for young children. A typical nurture classroom represents a safe, homely environment where critical play opportunities missed by the child in earlier years can be compensated for. In this therapeutic context, play can function alongside the curriculum and the adult's role is to meet the child's emotional needs while supporting the child's learning. There is a degree of flexibility as the child can move between directed curriculum activities and undirected play.

## Parental perspectives of emotional benefits of play for children

Most parents accept that children express their emotions while playing. An unpublished study conducted in the London Borough of Tower Hamlets (Sayeed and Guerin 1999) involving a sample of ten sets of parents of nursery-aged children from a range of cultural backgrounds produced the following results:

- 33% of parents defined their child's play in terms of his/her enjoyment.
- 90% of parents felt that children expressed their emotions through play.
- 80% of parents cited anger as the most commonly expressed emotion observed in their child's play.
- 100% of parents acknowledged that they should play with their children, mainly to provide emotional support and boost their child's confidence.

Over the recent decades, sociological changes such as the role of parents, mothers in particular, have resulted in different family structures. These changes are a direct consequence of industrialisation in Europe and North America and indirectly in some developing countries in Asia, Africa and South America. Nowadays, caregiving has become and is perceived to be a shared responsibility between two parents. With more women in the workplace and opportunities for working from home, the focus on the mother as the main caregiver has shifted to shared caregiving by both parents.

Due to practical reasons other caregivers such as childminders and nannies are employed by parents and play an essential role in the child's life. In some sections of society where the benefits of early years play provision have been recognised there has been an increase in the expectation that provision is made available by the state. In affluent countries with child-centred policies, statutory or voluntary bodies provide these facilities. This situation has resulted in many young children being cared for by trained or untrained caregivers rather than parents. Consequently, changes have resulted in different play relationships and interactions between the child and the caregiver with implications for the child's emotional development and play.

In some traditional societies children tend to be cared for as part of a group rather than as individuals. Konner (1977) found that amongst the Kong Bushmen of the Kalahari Desert where mothers return to work when their children are one year old, these children formed strong attachments to older children and adults. Findings from the Kibbutz study by N. Fox (1977) suggested that children benefited from being cared for by several adults in communal nurseries.

Care by adults beyond the family home has implications for a child's emotional responses to play and his/her long-term emotional development which is contingent upon the child's individuality and the quality of care.

Under these circumstances the child needs to:

- forge new relationships, which can result in positive or negative emotional responses;

- learn to differentiate his/her feelings for his/her main caregiver within the home and other caregivers outside;
- feel supported by and trust other caregivers.

This also has implications for parents who need to:

- extend their emotional bond with the child in trusting others to provide emotional stability and support for their child;
- deal with the child's emotional needs indirectly, i.e. through the other caregivers;
- feel the need to spend quality time with their children to compensate for lost caregiving time.

The most important aspects of caregiving are the type and quality of the relationship between the child and the carer, regardless of who is in the role of carer. Quality care should include opportunities for play so that the child can explore, discover and problem-solve making use of his/her imagination, creativity and skills.

Safe, secure relationships with parents or significant adults anchor the child's emotional wellbeing and development. Where childhood experiences are negative and relationships are fragile, play can act as medium for healing and bring about changes in the child's emotional growth and consequently in all areas of his/her functioning.

# Chapter 5

# Play in the SEN arena

*Michael flits from one activity to another . . . he can't seem to play for as long as the other children . . . while the other children are lining up to go out to play he is still putting on his coat . . . he doesn't seem to know what to do next and often requires adult support.*

The above is an excerpt from a consultation between a nursery teacher and an educational psychologist. Michael had been registered as having special educational needs at Stage 3 under the Code of Practice (DfE 1994) due to concerns about his learning and behaviour. Unless significant adults have knowledge and an understanding of Michael's needs and the contexts where these arise, it is unlikely that he will access suitable play and learning opportunities.

During the 1970s and 1980s there were rapid developments in the field of Special Educational Needs (SEN). It became clear to professionals that the child's potential can only be understood within the context where he/she learns. Labelling children's 'handicaps' was criticised and abandoned as it was accepted that SEN occurred as part of a continuum, from those children with more severe difficulties to those with less.

According to the most recent guidelines, the *Code of Practice on the Identification and Assessment of Special Educational Needs* (DfE 1994), SEN is defined as:

A child has Special Educational Needs if he or she has learning difficulty which calls for special educational provision to be made for him/her.

A child has a learning difficulty if he/she:

(a) has a significantly greater difficulty in learning than the majority of children of the same age.
(b) has a disability, which either hinders or prevents the child from making use of educational facilities of a kind provided for children of the same age in schools within the area of the local education authority.

(c) is under five and falls within the definition at (a) or (b) above and would do if special educational provision was not made for the child.

The child must not be regarded as having a learning difficulty solely because the language or form of language of the home is different from the language in which he or she is or will be taught.

Special educational provision means:

(a) for a child over two, educational provision which is additional to, or otherwise different from, the educational provision made for children of the child's age in maintained schools, other than special schools.
(b) for a child under two, educational provision of any kind.

   (Section 156, p.5)

The Code of Practice is due to be revised for implementation during 2001.

In the past children with SEN were commonly confused with children 'in need'. The Children Act (1989) defines children in need as:

* those unlikely to achieve or maintain, or have the opportunity of achieving or maintaining, a reasonable standard of health or development without the provision of services;
* those whose health or development is likely to be significantly impaired, or further impaired, without the provision of such services;
* those who are disabled.

Children 'in need' may not have SEN but the 'slippery slope' phenomenon can arise if appropriate provisions are not made.

The definition of SEN emphasises the child's difficulty accessing learning but is non-specific about the cause and specific problem. The return to categories of SEN in the Code of Practice enables educators to identify, assess, plan and provide for children with special educational needs. The categories applicable to young children are as follows:

* learning difficulties
* emotional and behavioural difficulties
* physical disabilities
* sensory impairments (visual/hearing)
* speech and language difficulties
* medical conditions.

The continuum within each of these categories cannot be overlooked as it has direct implications for how a child's individual needs can be met.

These categories and corresponding criteria have provided clarity and guidance to schools where statutory assessments for a small number of children need to be considered by the Local Education Authority (LEA).

## Play and inclusion

In the UK, the Warnock Report (DES 1978) was the catalyst for legislative change in the realm of SEN. Since the 1981 Education Act the inclusion of children with SEN in their mainstream school has been a pertinent issue. While it has been recognised that this is the right of a child with SEN to be educated alongside his/her mainstream peers, it continues to be a challenge for education providers and other agencies as well as a dilemma for parents. The Green Paper for SEN (DfEE 1998) has put forward the strongest argument to date in favour of inclusive education, highlighting the need for early assessment and intervention by early years providers.

The Warnock Report valued the potential of nursery education for supporting the development of young children including those with SEN. It was advocated that provision should be increased to offer equal access to provision for all pre-schoolers.

In recent years the status of early years education has heightened. This is also true for children with SEN. This has happened as a consequence of special needs legislation and increased provision, i.e. more children are being cared for and educated outside the home at an earlier age and for longer periods of time in school nurseries, day nurseries, play groups and family centres. This has resulted in growing skills and expertise on the part of early years providers and practitioners. In England and Wales a child with a Statement of SEN can start compulsory education at as young as two years.

Throughout changes in guidance and provision the value of play for young children has been in evidence. A visitor to any early years setting can immediately observe play activities and should sense a play ethos. The extent to which play activities are structured and directed is variable. If an early years setting is offering various play opportunities including exploratory, creative, imaginative, physical, problem-solving, social and free-flow play to take place, one can only assume that children are playing for pleasure and they are learning and developing at their own pace. It is widely acknowledged that play is essential for every child's healthy all-round development and it is just as valuable for a child with special educational needs.

In the UK, more than ever, young children with SEN are to be found in early years settings outside the home. As far as possible all children in the early years should have their needs met in mainstream provision. However, a small percentage (less than 3 per cent approx.) of all children require high levels of care and expertise and may need early access to specialist provision. Sometimes the extent of a child's special educational needs has yet to be identified, or as increasingly is the case with early identification and assessment, young children with SEN are found in mainstream inclusive settings. The Green Paper (1998) describes inclusion as a process rather than a fixed state. It stresses that as far as possible all pupils with SEN should be educated in mainstream schools with full participation in the curriculum and general activities.

Consideration of inclusive education issues seems to be more progressive in the USA. The Americans with Disabilities Act (ADA) emphasises the need for safe inclusion in educational, recreational and work settings, without prescribing exactly how this can be achieved. Issues such as safety and developmental appropriateness of activities need to be addressed in play environments. The key characteristics of inclusive play environments were described by Winter *et al.* (1994). They identified three fundamental components of inclusion which apply to children's play:

- access – the child can enter the intended environment;
- activity – the child can participate actively;
- variability – the child can choose from a variety of play activities.

According to the International Association for the Child's Right to Play (IPA) every child has a right to play. Its 1977 declaration includes the idea that play, along with the basic needs of children, is vital to development of the potential of *all* children. The process of achieving safe inclusion needs to be endorsed by legislation, research and commitment through practice. In the UK there is a long journey ahead.

Research around play and its importance for children with SEN is limited and inconclusive. Studies tend to focus on within-child types of SEN, e.g. Down's Syndrome or on children with sensory impairments. These findings are often ungeneralisable across wider groups of children with SEN and do not account for individual differences within these groups. Bailey and Wolery (1989) looked at the factors that made children 'special' and concluded that the causes of SEN fell into three groups: biological factors, environmental conditions and unknown causes.

While there is increasing emphasis on measuring and monitoring the learning of young children, for the child with SEN his/her potential rather than performance should be the focus of the play provider.

The outcome of a child's play experience is often contingent upon the adult's expectations of the child's ability or potential to play. Consideration needs to be given to plans made to meet the child's needs and address the challenges that may affect implementation of these plans. The play environment needs to be assessed and monitored to encourage safe play. The role of adults needs to be clearly defined as it is central to the development of children's play, especially those with SEN who may need adult involvement. Play outcomes can be desirable or undesirable depending on the type and quality of adult involvement and provision (see Figure 5.1).

In order for the play experience to be a success for the child with SEN the following four areas need to be a focus for play providers.

## Expectations

Fundamentally the play provider must understand, appreciate and advocate the value of play for young children. When a child with SEN is the focus of play, the adult will naturally set expectations about how the child can/will play.

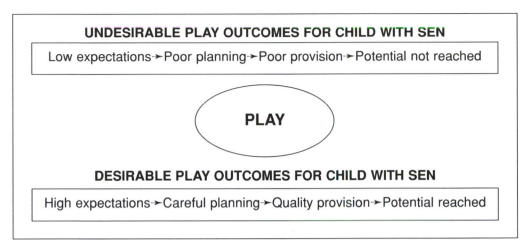

**Figure 5.1** Adult-supported play outcomes for children with SEN

Sometimes expectations can be inaccurate (too high or too low), affecting the process and product of the play experience and the adult–child relationship.

To cite for example, an adult offered only exploratory play activities to a young language-impaired child. This was based on the adult's assumption that because the child did not use or understand language effectively his functioning was generally at a low level. In fact at home this child was capable of and experienced with problem-solving tasks such as fitting shapes in a post-box and completing simple puzzles.

For all children, especially those with SEN, providers need to collect some basic data about the child (e.g. medical information) and his/her context (relevant home and other factors). Information about the child's strengths and weaknesses should be gathered by the play provider from parents, carers and other professionals who know the child best. This process should allow the play provider to arrive at more specific and individualised expectations for the child. The play provider may wish to conduct a baseline of the child's functioning in terms of his/her play skills. The authors' model of play-based assessment in Chapter 6 should give some guidance regarding relevant areas of the child's development.

### Planning

When the adult analyses and makes sense of the information gathered through observation and/or involvement in the child's play this allows him/her to determine expectations for the child. This process also supports appropriate planning of long-term goals and short-term targets in identified areas of need.

### Long-term goals
These need to refer to the general context where the child is placed, e.g. a nursery curriculum or the play opportunities available in the home. However, they need to be drawn up for the individual child with reference to his/her present play skills

and future play potential. The allocated time-scale for review of the programme and re-assessment of the child's needs could take place at 3- to 6-month intervals. The planning and reviewing process may depend on the complexity of the child's SEN and the context in which he/she is being assessed and supported.

*Short-term targets*

Individualised play targets should be drawn up and re-visited on a weekly basis. Collaboration with parents and other professionals can lead to suggestions to be included. These can be recorded on an Individual Play Plan (IPP). This format emphasises the interactionist nature of play between adult and child. It enables the adult to monitor the child's progress with play through direct contact. Ongoing reviews identify changes and progress, which can inform target-setting.

The IPP could take the following form:

| Name of child:<br><br>Name of play provision: | | Date of birth:<br><br>Named play provider: | |
|---|---|---|---|
| Play target(s)<br>Date | Resources/<br>Environment | Adult–child<br>Interaction | Play outcome<br>Date |
|  |  |  |  |

**Figure 5.2** Individual Play Plan

This IPP format can be used in conjunction with the authors' Play Based Assessment Summary sheet to plan for children with SEN in the next chapter.

## Environment/provision

As play providers adults must be aware of the importance of examining the play environment before assuming a child with SEN has a play deficit. The play of all children is affected by the physical and social environment and according to Hughes *et al.* (1998) play behaviour must be separated from the child's potential for play as some environments are more conducive to play for children with SEN than others. Newson (1993) emphasised that one cannot assume that a child cannot do an activity without the chance to try it under a variety of conditions, over time and using a range of equipment.

The physical environment refers to the time allocation, the arrangement of space, resources (e.g. staffing) and equipment available. Safety is central to the inclusion of children with SEN: without this, children will not have the freedom to explore, create and take risks like their mainstream peers. In order for activities to be safe they should be developmentally appropriate and challenging. In larger childcare/nursery settings training around safety issues is necessary to inclusive practice. Ideally information should be disseminated across provisions but it may be necessary to include a maintenance programme, e.g. regular supervision and training of childcare workers, to uphold standards. Consultation with professionals such as physiotherapists, occupational therapists and other specialists may yield valuable guidance to ensure the comfort, safety and equality of opportunity for play (Eichinger and Woltman 1993).

In considering the child's social environment issues such as age, gender and culture of peers and adults need to be taken into account. Relationships and interactions within the play setting should support an optimal display of his/her potential. If a child feels relaxed and valued he/she is more likely to engage in, initiate and sustain play.

### *Role of adults/others*

In relation to the play of children with SEN adults have two roles:

- Indirect involvement: the play provider plans and provides play opportunities. This role may not require the adult to be directly involved with the child. As mentioned previously the adult has a central role in gathering information and using this to plan for the child's specific play needs. This is particularly relevant to children joining a new play setting with previous involvement from other professionals, e.g. where a child has already been subject to a multi-professional assessment at a Child Development Centre.
- Direct involvement: the play provider assesses, plans and provides play opportunities. In some cases the play provider may gather information from others as well as conducting his/her own assessment through participation in child's play in the play setting in order to plan for the child's play needs.

### Providing play for children with identified SEN

Play amongst young children with SEN can be more easily understood through informed case examples. The authors have chosen to explore this area with reference to the categories of SEN in the Code of Practice (DfE 1994), followed by analysis and discussion.

Case examples will be used to illustrate the types of special needs and how the child's SEN affects their play. They are based on the authors' observations but the names of the children have been changed to ensure confidentiality. They have a 'fly on the wall' quality and are not intended to explore background or within-child issues. The focus of each case study is the child's play in context. In each case the reader has an opportunity to consider the following questions in an analysis of each case:

- What are the issues for the child?
- What helps the child's play?

- What hinders the child's play?
- What needs to be done to help the child's play to develop?

## A. General learning difficulties

The vast majority of children with SEN have general learning difficulties and consequently their play requires planning and support.

> Their general level of academic attainment will be significantly below that of their peers. In most cases, they will have difficulty acquiring basic literacy and numeracy skills and many will have speech and language difficulties. Some may also have poor social skills and may show signs of emotional and behavioural difficulties.                    (Code of Practice, DfE 1994 p. 54)

---

**Case Example: Sophie, a five-year old girl with Down's Syndrome**
Tommy, Paula, William and Sophie are playing 'Follow the leader' in the nursery playground. Their play seems to be sequenced in three steps – walking on a balance beam, followed by crawling through a tunnel and finally using the slide.
Tommy: I'm first.
Paula:    No, I'm the leader.
William queues up behind Paula.
Tommy: Come on everyone. Come on Sophie.
Sophie looks around, smiles.
Paula:    Are you playing, Sophie?
Sophie slowly but eagerly lines up behind Paula. The other children in their turn start the circuit. When the other three children have completed Sophie remains cautiously standing on the beam. She stumbles as she looks ahead to see where the others are but they are lining up behind her again.
Paula:    Hurry up Sophie.
Sophie gets off the beam and moves to the end of the queue again.
Sophie:  Miss, Miss (to her Learning Support Assistant (LSA)).
Her LSA approaches her and holds her hand, steadying Sophie on the beam. Sophie walks across the beam with a broad smile. Her LSA asks Sophie 'What should you do next?' Sophie looks blankly.
William: Sophie come in the tunnel, it's good, it's dark.
Sophie hesitates and pulls her LSA towards the tunnel.
Sophie:  You come Miss.
LSA:      No, you go in, I will stand outside. Sophie gestures back to the beam.

---

Sophie's sociability and enthusiasm enable her to participate in the group play activity. However, her gross motor skills, particularly balance, hinder her participation at the level of her peers. Her level of learning difficulty prevents her from using cognitive skills such as imitating her peers and sequencing her play without adult support. Sophie's apparent lack of experience as well as her limited skills may be affecting her confidence in this play situation. Access to higher functioning peers and adult support complements Sophie's scope for developing her play further. In the past it was assumed that children with learning difficulties neither wanted nor needed to play (McConkey 1985). This is no longer accepted as the case. While there are obvious variations in levels of functioning and skills, play can act as a positive learning process. In the case of children with Down's Syndrome research by Sigman and Sena (1993) has shown that this group are more interested in looking at stimuli than exploring in a multi-sensory way. In Sophie's case she seemed more comfortable in the role of observer than participant. According to Faulkener and Lewis (1995) the development of children with Down's Syndrome is different from that of normally developing children, not just delayed. Although their deficits in the areas of short-term auditory memory and motivation should not significantly affect their play, their delayed responses to language should be taken into account by supporting adults. Children with general learning difficulties tend to develop their play skills along the same continuum as their more able peers but at a slower rate. Wing *et al.* (1977) confirmed this view in relation to symbolic play. Thus the supporting adult and more able peers are crucial to the provision of play opportunities and play development.

## B. Emotional and behavioural difficulties

According to the Code of Practice (DfE 1994 p. 58) pupils with emotional and behavioural difficulties 'fail to meet expectations in school and in some but by no means all cases may also disrupt the education of others'.

---

**Case Example: Amanda, four and a half years, is looked after by a childminder**

Amanda is playing with Lego on the carpet. As soon as she hears the voices of other children in the next room she gathers the pieces together.

Johnnie:  Let's play Lego.

Amanda: These are mine. You can't have them.

Johnnie and Carl start to play with the miniature garage. Amanda glances in their direction.

Carl:        Amanda is coming.

After a couple of minutes she approaches them. Amanda reaches across the two younger boys, grabs the cars and breaks their model.

Johnnie:    Barbara, it's Amanda (calling to child minder).

Barbara:    Please give the cars back, Amanda and play together.

Amanda:    No, they (cars) go with the Lego.

Amanda can play independently when following her own agenda. She can communicate her intentions, even though she does not always choose the most appropriate means. Her difficulties surface in relation to other children sharing her space and equipment. Her brash approach to play is known to her peers and she confirms her disruptive reputation with them and the supervising adult. Does she know how to share her toys and play cooperatively? For some children, like Amanda, the development of play skills is not incidental and cannot be taken for granted. Adult anticipation of the difficulties in the play situation might have prevented some conflict. Unfortunately Amanda's positive play was not identified or rewarded. She could have benefited from adult modelling, e.g. a substituted response for her grabbing behaviour.

There is an understandable reluctance for young children to be labelled as having emotional and behavioural difficulties. Why is this the case?

- Children are perceived as too young to develop such difficult behaviour.
- Their behaviours can be interpreted as 'phases'.
- Contextual factors in the child's home or play provision attribute responsibility to significant adults.

Regardless of the causality, the outcome of the presenting needs has direct implications for the development of the child's play skills, which are funda-mental to the child's overall development. The context for a child's play must support his/her needs. The following principles suggested by Andreski and Nicholls (1993) based on a child's needs can be used to establish a policy to support his/her social development. They can be applied effectively in the home or other play settings:

- love and care
- security
- adequate rest and sleep
- freedom to explore
- importance of self-image
- adult as a role model
- consistency in treatment
- opportunities for self-expression
- opportunities for learning
- boundaries to behaviour.

Where active intervention is needed to provide boundaries for children's behaviour, principles of behavioural psychology can offer useful strategies. These approaches can be used by parents and professionals through 'examining problem situations and agreeing strategies for change which are individualised, context-related and involve minimum intervention' (White and Cameron 1987). This approach is used in the Portage Early Education Programme (Unit 8 p. 3). This is known simply as the ABC of Behaviour (Antecedents – Background – Consequences). The events leading up to the behaviour, the context for the behaviour and how the behaviour was dealt with by others (positive or negative response) need to be given careful consideration to analyse the problem objectively and plan for change.

### Attention deficit and hyperactivity disorder (ADHD)

A working party of the British Psychological Society in 1996 produced an extensive report on the subject of ADHD called 'Attention Deficit Hyperactivity Disorder (ADHD): A Psychological Response to an Evolving Concept'. The report refers to a small group of children described as impulsive, overactive and/or inattentive to the extent that it is atypical for their developmental age and is a significant obstacle to their social and educational success.

Most of the research in this area has been conducted in the USA. Alessandri (1991) looked at the play of pre-school children with ADHD and concluded that their peer play was less sophisticated and they were less attentive and cooperative during structured play activities. An apparent lack of social skills, including insulting and critical comments towards peers, limited their opportunities for play. However their social skills rather than play skills are the main difficulty and can be addressed through social skills training which for young children can be taught through social play activities.

### Abused and neglected children

This group refers to children who are known to have been abused emotionally, physically and sexually and/or neglected in terms of their basic needs. Alessandri (1991) showed that the play of abused children differs from that of non-abused children in that they played less maturely in their imaginative, cognitive, social and fantasy play.

Anatomically correct dolls have been used to investigate sexual abuse in young children. However, this approach was questioned by Cohn (1991) as he found that most children played in ways that could be interpreted as sexual with these dolls. If the special needs of this group of children are not addressed this may have implications for the development of their learning and play skills. Many of these children could be considered as suitable candidates for play therapy or nurture groups.

## C. Physical disability

A child's physical difficulties may be the result of an illness or injury, which might have short- or long-term consequences, or may arise from a congenital condition. Such difficulties may, without action by the school or the LEA, limit the child's access to the full curriculum. Some children with physical disabilities may also have sensory impairments, neurological problems and learning difficulties.                    (Code of Practice, DfE 1994 p. 61)

> **Case Example: Tim, three years old, has cerebral palsy affecting the movement of all four limbs. His head movement is also restricted.**
>
> Tim is sitting in his pushchair next to a table. His teacher approaches with a cause-and-effect sound toy in the shape of a teddy.
>
> Teacher: Here you are...you like this teddy don't you? Let's Tickle the Teddy!
>
> As soon as the teacher touches the tummy of the teddy a giggling sound is heard. Tim jerks his body with excitement and smiles.
>
> Teacher: Good boy Tim.
>
> She moves the teddy closer to him and helps him to press the teddy with his elbow. A sound is produced.
>
> Teacher: Well done Tim, let's try again.
>
> The teddy is placed under his elbow and Tim sways his body, pressing his elbow on the teddy's tummy. A giggling sound is produced.
>
> Teacher: Clever boy, you can do it!

Tim seems motivated to play by having access to equipment that is suited to his individual needs. Tim had direct support from his teacher based on modelling and repetition. The teacher's feedback was consistent and contingent upon his positive responses. On the other hand he was entirely reliant on skilled adult support in his play. Tim's physical restriction impedes his exploration of the play environment and may be affecting different kinds and levels of play skills. Thus, in order to set appropriate expectations his play potential needs to be established in consultation with relevant professionals (e.g. physiotherapists, occupational therapists, speech therapists) and parents.

Across the continuum of physical disability access to the environment is the main hindrance to the development of play. While it is possible that an able child could be trapped in a disabled body and deprived of opportunities to progress, physical disability can go hand in hand with other SEN. Where a physically disabled child has difficulty communicating either verbally or non-verbally, there are direct implications for the development of play skills. Davies (1985) described how many children with cerebral palsy have visual perceptual difficulties.

In the case of this group of children multi-agency assessment is recommended. The SCOPE model as outlined in M. Fox (1997) offers useful suggestions for an approach to assessment.

## D. Sensory impairments (hearing)

A significant proportion of children has some degree of hearing difficulties. Hearing losses may be temporary or permanent. Temporary hearing losses are usually caused by the condition known as 'glue ear' which occurs most often in the early years. Such hearing losses fluctuate and may be mild or moderate in degree. They can seriously compound other learning difficulties... Permanent hearing losses are usually sensory-neural and vary from mild through moderate, severe or profound. Children with severe or profound hearing loss may have severe or complex communication difficulties'

(DfE Code of Practice 1994. p. 62)

---

**Case Example: Fiona, a five year old girl whose hearing is under specialist investigation.**

In the corner of the nursery class a group of 4–5 year old boys and girls are busy making a structure with wooden bricks. Fiona is watching their game from a distance.

Teacher: Fiona, you go and help them.

Fiona doesn't respond.
Laura, another child, runs to Fiona.

Laura:    You come and play with us. Fiona smiles and walks towards the children.

Laura hands a brick to Fiona.

Laura:    You make the kitchen and I make the kitchen.
Joseph:  No, she can't play.
Nina:     She can't talk.

Fiona throws the brick at the structure.

Nina and others: Miss, Miss, it's Fiona.

Fiona runs to the other side of the nursery and starts to cry.

---

Fiona appears curious and observant in the context of her peers' play. However her hearing loss prevents her from understanding the play context and responding to her teacher's suggestion. She can accept an invitation from a supportive playmate but seems entirely unable to cope with criticism. Her lack of confidence and poor communication skills prevent her from challenging others and asserting herself. The adult support in this case needed to be sustained in order for Fiona's peer interactions to be positive.

There is a wide range of children with hearing impairments attending a range of play settings. These include children whose hearing loss has been diagnosed, others who are under investigation and those with suspected impairments. These have direct implications for the development of communication skills. In their play, hearing-impaired children are less engaged in symbolic and socio-dramatic play (Esposito and Koorland 1989). In the case of young children, inclusive play provision can offer rich and sophisticated models of play behaviours. In the aforementioned study children in integrated provision engaged in more cooperative play and those in segregated provision engaged in more parallel play. In the UK in recent years, the London Borough of Newham's Education Authority has taken positive steps to include young children with hearing impairments in mainstream settings (Robinson 1997).

## E. Sensory impairment (visual)

Visual difficulties take many forms with widely differing implications for child's education. They range from relatively minor and remediable conditions to total blindness. Some children are born blind; other lose their sight partially or completely, as a result of accidents or illness. In some cases visual impairment is one of multiple disability. Whatever the cause of the child's visual impairment, the major issue in identifying and assessing the child's special educational needs will relate to the degree and nature of functional vision, partial sight or blindness, and the child's ability to adapt socially and psychologically as well as to progress in an educational context.'                    (Code of Practice, DfE 1994 p. 64)

---

**Case Example: Leo, aged three years, who is totally blind.**

Leo is helped onto a tricycle by his Learning Support Assistant (LSA). He has seated himself appropriately, holding the handlebars with his feet on the pedals. His LSA moves away to encourage his independence. He pedals forward and a pillar obstructs his movement. He tries hard to pedal forward and tries with his feet on the ground but without success. After a couple of minutes he puts his feet back on the pedals and pedals backwards. He perseveres with this until the tricycle wheels touch the wall behind him. His discovery of available space led to him speeding forward. His LSA sees him, leaps forward and holds the bicycle. She anxiously says 'Don't go too fast, you'll hurt yourself.'

---

Leo purposefully engages in exploring space available to him through problem-solving and employing his well-developed physical skills. The extent to which he can access and explore the play environment safely is central to the development of his play skills. Peer involvement in Leo's play is lacking. A sensitive and experienced adult can create opportunities for cooperative and social play and offer the scope for extension of play beyond the solitary stage.

There are many misconceptions around the play of blind and partially-sighted children. According to research conducted by Missiuna and Pollock (1991) the stereotype that blind children cannot or will not play is a secondary disability.

However there are some differences between how blind/partially-sighted children play in comparison with their sighted peers. In Hughes *et al.* (1998) it was shown that the play behaviours for visually-impaired children were predominantly exploratory and sensory-motor. This contrasted significantly with a very small percentage of time spent engaged in symbolic play. In this study the partially-sighted children relied on their residual vision and other senses. In the case of blind children a study by Tait (1973) showed that although the blind children can engage in highly imaginative play they do so less often than their sighted peers. Skellenger and Hill (1994) suggested that children with a visual impairment in an inclusive play setting require adult facilitation to understand their level of play and make it meaningful for them.

## F. Speech and language difficulties

Although most speech and language difficulties will have been identified before a child reaches school, some children will have significant speech and language difficulties, which impair their ability to participate in the classroom by the time they start school. This may in turn have serious consequences for the child's academic attainment and also give rise to emotional and behavioural difficulties.                    (Code of Practice, DfE 1994 p. 66)

---

**Case Example: Ben, aged four years, currently undergoing assessment at the Speech and Language Therapy Service.**

Five children aged four to five years are playing in the corner of a Children's Centre base room.

Tommy: I am Miss Kelly (his key-worker). You all sit down.

Other children sit on the carpet facing Tommy as his class of pupils.

Tommy: Don't talk. We do singing. It's your turn, you sing (pointing to Joanna).

Joanna sings 'Twinkle, Winkle...'

Tommy: Clap hands.

Others clap.

Tommy: It's your turn Ben, you do it.

Ben looks nervous but tries to hum the tune of the same song.

Poppy:  That's not it, Ben can't sing, he can't play.

Tommy: Yes he can play, clap hands for him.

---

Ben is a willing and engaging player in this game of school in spite of his delayed speech and language. Until he needed to make a verbal contribution in this play situation his difficulties would probably have gone unchallenged. His peer support was variable: at one level support was forthcoming at the other extreme he was subjected to criticism. In this instance direct adult involvement could risk changing the dynamics of the game unless he or she is a skilled participator.

Much of the literature tends to focus on a distinction between a language delay (slow rate but normal development) and a language disorder (uneven and atypical development). In the case of young children this distinction is often unclear and can only be clarified through ongoing and multi-disciplinary assessment and review (including parents, teacher, speech and language therapist and other professionals). Where children have delayed speech and language skills, environmental factors such as peer pressure can severely affect their participation in play activities, especially symbolic or socio-dramatic play. When children do not have the language to engage in make-believe play they are unlikely to develop this form of play (McCune 1986). Focused adult intervention is needed to break this cycle.

## G. Medical condition

Some medical conditions may, if appropriate action is not taken, have a significant impact on the child's academic attainment and/or may give rise to emotional and behavioural difficulties. Some of the commonest medical conditions are likely to be congenital heart disease, epilepsy, asthma, cystic fibrosis, haemophilia, sickle cell anaemia, diabetes, renal failure, eczema, rheumatoid disorders, and leukaemia and childhood cancers.

(Code of Practice, DfE 1994 p. 67)

---

**Case Example: Aaron, aged five years, with a diagnosis of cystic fibrosis.**
Danny, Jason, Forhad, Chi and Aaron are lining up to race from one end of the nursery playground to the other.

Jason: Ready, steady, go!

All run, Aaron stops halfway, out of breath, while Chi looks behind him. He returns to Aaron.

Chi:    Let me pull you fast.
Jason: You are cheating.
Chi to Aaron: Let's sit down.
Chi to others: We don't want to run ... we are judges.

---

In spite of his motivation and popularity, Aaron's health prevented him participating as fully as his playmates. His able peer's awareness and understanding of Aaron's medical condition created a role for him as a judge, enabling the play sequence to continue. For children with an obvious medical condition in a supportive setting, peer empathy may be more forthcoming than in the case of other kinds of special educational needs.

In their paper 'Creating play environments for children with special needs', Winter *et al.* (1994) emphasised the importance of safety for children with SEN. Clear information is especially essential for the access of children with medical needs. The implications of medical conditions on a child's play opportunities can only can be ascertained in consultation with other professionals, especially medical professionals.

## H. Childhood autism

Childhood autism does not feature in the current Code of Practice (1994) as a category of SEN. However as a group of children with complex and individual-ised needs which are difficult to assess and meet, separate guidelines will be provided in the revised Code of Practice.

---

**Case Example: Fatima, aged four years, with a diagnosis of an autistic spectrum disorder.**

Fatima charges into the front room of the family home. She goes directly to the video rack, ignoring her brother, Imran. She gathers 5–6 videotapes in their cases from the rack and starts to line them up on the floor in front of the television. While her brother is watching 'Teletubbies' her presence obscures his view of the TV screen.

Imran: This is mine, give my video.

Fatima does not look at him or object when he grabs one of the videotapes and shouts:

Imran: I want my Teletubbies. (Pointing to the case for the videotape)

Fatima makes a throaty sound and keeps rearranging her videos. She is totally absorbed in her own play.

Father: Imran, leave her alone, she's playing her game.

---

Fatima presents as having many of the characteristics of an autistic spectrum disorder. She appears to concentrate well on her chosen activity. She is busy with her own play, ignoring the presence of her brother and not showing any interest in the 'Teletubbies' programme. She does not respond to her brother through eye contact or verbally, engrossing herself in a repetitive activity. The communicative intent of her throaty sounds is unclear. From her father's intervention it appears that in the home context Fatima's solitary play behaviour is accepted and taken for granted.

It is generally perceived that understanding and planning for children with autism is challenging. Several misconceptions exist in terms of their learning and play behaviour. Contrary to the general views about the repetitive nature of play among children with autism, Quinn and Rubin (1984) found that this was not always the case. Even able autistic children engage less frequently in symbolic play than other children. However, the reasons for this have been attributed to their motivation to play symbolically (Lewis and Boucher 1988). Although the disordered language development of this group of children cannot be over-looked as a reason for their ability to play symbolically.

The play medium offers limitless opportunities to understand and intervene with a child on the autistic spectrum. A safe, familiar play environment provides unthreatening play experiences for the child. Newson (1993) describes how play can be used as an assessment technique in specialist settings.

The case examples above aim to illustrate how children with SEN can function in the play situation. However, these individual cases cannot embrace the continuum of need within each category of SEN. To ensure equality of opportunity, play providers should have an inclusive philosophy, which translates to practice, such that they establish the play requirements of the child and take appropriate steps to address identified strengths and weaknesses.

# Chapter 6

# Play-based assessment

Play is a child's natural and spontaneous behaviour where he/she can express his/her wants and needs. Due to the familiar and unthreatening nature of play, children can perform to the best of their abilities in the play setting. Play can offer an opportunity for an interactive experience with peers and adults. Play has the potential to be used by parents, carers and professionals to assess the functioning of young children.

Historically, parents and professionals from educational and non-educational agencies have assessed young children using informal approaches. In the UK, the increasing use of pre-baseline assessments in nursery classes and Early Learning Goals as objectives has placed an onus on early years providers to conduct early assessments. Formalised baseline assessments in reception classes are another indicator of the growing need to establish a marker for a child's functioning at a specific time in their early education. The baseline is followed by the statutory Standard Assessment Tasks (SATs) for pupils aged 7 years. Consequently, teachers and early years staff are having to develop skills of assessment to meet the needs of very young children in educational and non-educational settings. Parents and professionals have to acquire a clear understanding of these assessments, and the implications for the child's learning.

## Establishing a child's strengths and weaknesses

The concept of assessment as a means of identifying a child's strengths and weaknesses has shifted from a theoretical idea to practice. It has specific significance for educators as provision for children should be dependent on their identified needs, and consequently for the majority of children assessment has become an integral part of their education. Assessment can be defined as the identification of the present level of a child's functioning/development through observation/interaction with an adult in order to understand and meet the child's needs. The Task Group on Assessment and Testing (TGAT) (DES

1988) stated that 'Assessment is at the heart of the process of providing for children's learning.'

Purposeful assessment in a structured setting can take the form of:

- providing information which adults can apply to take the child's learning forward (formative and diagnostic);
- providing evidence of the knowledge and understanding of the child (summative);
- providing information for the adult to adapt the learning environment to suit the child (evaluative);
- providing a medium of communication between parents and significant adults in relation to the child's progress (informative). (DES 1988)

Over time professionals have become increasingly skilled at measuring progress and performance of individuals, hence formalised measurement and quantitative analysis have evolved. The two main techniques for assessment are frequently used:

- Norm-referenced assessment: A measure of particular ability based on a comparison between the individual and a group of the same age and background. This is otherwise known as a standardised assessment technique.
- Criterion-referenced assessment: The identification of an individual's current level of functioning in terms of the skills needed to complete a task or set of tasks.

Normative tests have been criticised on the grounds that the result of such testing does not directly inform planning for the child. Limitations of psychometric measurements include their accessibility only to certain professionals, their low predictive value as well as cultural and contextual biases (Cummins 1984). Criterion-referenced assessments have also been challenged due to the linear and compartmentalised view of development that they represent. Other assessment methods such as interviews, reports and checklists can be used to support observational or adult directed play-based assessment. According to Wolfendale (1993) assessment should:

- have a clear purpose
- be ongoing
- include parent(s)
- reflect cultural and linguistic background.

## Assessment of young children

In the home context, assessment is an integral part of parents' and significant adults' interactions with the child. Generally toys and playthings are chosen by parents, relatives and friends usually on an approximate age-related basis and with children's developmental needs in mind. Instinctively and continuously, carers assess the child's behaviour in order to help him/her grow and develop. As the child's world radically widens to the classroom/playgroup/nursery the assessment process continues such that his/her needs can be met in different contexts. The role of the teacher/nursery staff as assessors during the early years is crucial. In general terms and more particularly in the case of children with SEN, early assessment provides a baseline from which the quality and rate of learning can be measured and progress monitored effectively.

Whereas assessment for older children can take the form of traditional testing including formal tasks and examinations, young children are unlikely to perform to their potential under these conditions. Younger children are more likely to have difficulty physically accessing activities, understanding standardised instructions, offering verbal responses and coping with unfamiliar materials. Play has the potential to overcome these obstacles. However when assessing young children using informal methods such as play, which is very accessible to the child, adults need to be aware of what they are looking for and why.

Where children have been identified as having special educational needs, the Code of Practice (1994) emphasises the need for early assessment by including guidelines for assessment of children less than two years old. In the case of children less than five years old it suggests that assessment should focus on the level of development of the child in the following areas: physical health and function, communication skills, perceptual and motor skills, self-help skills, social skills, emotional/behavioural development and responses to learning experiences.

In his article entitled 'Who Knows Me Best?', Newton (1988) suggested that pre-school assessment sets out to understand a child's functioning and learning skills, behaviour and general development with a view to facilitating and improving these. Assessment should be a process over time, which enables the assessor to formulate a fuller picture of the child's strengths and weaknesses.

## Assessment through play

As play is a spontaneous and voluntary behaviour of a child according to Garvey (1991), it provides an opportunity for adults to interact with the child, understand his/her world and support his/her learning and development in all areas. Play embraces a range of activities and can be used effectively to assess all young children regardless of their abilities or potential.

Gaussen (1984) suggests that professionals who are working with children with impaired development need to look beyond developmental milestones. He describes an interactionist model of assessment of young children with learning difficulties in terms of the functioning of the child within his/her environment.

This model of assessment aims to:

- provide information on the child's current functioning
- act as a basis for intervention
- be used as a method for evaluating change.

He emphasises that the adult's interpretation of the child's action is the key to future intervention. In other words the assessor's own knowledge, skills and experience will have a bearing on the assessment and perceived strengths and weaknesses of the child.

Parents and professionals gather information about a child's functioning while he/she is playing. Approaches to assessment through play may take four forms:

- Child playing alone – adult observing
- Child playing with the other child/children – adult observing
- Child playing with adult – other adult(s) observing
- Child playing with adult as participator and assessor.

Newton (1988) endorsed the philosophy of Garfinkel (1967) who argued that one needs to be included in a situation in order to understand it. He applied this idea to the assessment of young children in his claim that along the continuum of assessment the richest information can be gathered by adults through observation and participation in children's play.

Newson (1993) recommended that criterion-referenced assessment should be used to achieve a full picture of the child through play. Her original play-based assessment was devised for the purpose of an assessment clinic which was adapted for assessment of children with SEN in a special needs classroom. Her model aimed to be entirely child-centred with a focus on the child's strengths as well as weaknesses. She emphasised the difference between general and specific areas of developmental delay, highlighted the importance of the child's disposition or 'personal pattern' and learning style. Partnership with parents included inviting their evidence from home to enrich the professionals' assessment. In the SEN classroom she suggested that observations should be organised and play materials should be selected carefully so that the outcome of the assessment is conclusive with a clear plan of action.

Judy Waters (1999) developed a model of play-based assessment called, 'Let's Play – A Guide to Interactive Assessment with Young Children'. Taking a dynamic assessment perspective, her approach aims to provide an interactive and flexible form of assessment for children with SEN. This technique enables the assessor to identify the child's approaches to learning in a familiar play situation in order to support future planning for the child. Her model will be referred to in Chapter 8.


## Development of play-based assessment (PBA)

In the pursuit of an interactive criterion-referenced approach to the assessment of young children the authors developed their model of PBA, initially through formalising their own practice. Its origin, development, form and application within the wider context was explored.

PBA has been developed as a result of practice and research. Three research studies by the authors informed the development of the current model. Two studies, carried out while the model was being developed, looked at parents' and teachers' views of play for young children. The authors felt that parents can be equal partners in the assessment process, particularly in the case of PBA, and with this view in mind the authors considered that parental views of play were very important. The other study specifically aimed to refine the model of PBA by establishing its effectiveness in qualitative terms. The participants of this study were Educational Psychologists in Training (EPiTs) and practising Educational Psychologists (EPs).

In 1995, a small sample of nursery staff and parents of Tower Hamlets, London were interviewed about their views of play, including its value, gender and cultural issues. Cultural influences on play were viewed as less significant than gender but it was established that play was viewed as central to adults' thinking around children's learning and development. Due to the size of the study it is unlikely that the results are generalisable beyond this sample.

The most recent research was conducted in 1999 in a nursery school in Tower Hamlets with a small group of volunteer parents. These volunteer parents were from diverse social, cultural, and linguistic backgrounds. This sample would be typical of many multicultural inner city areas. The authors wanted to gather parental views on children's play. In summary, there was a consensus that play was a valuable activity for young children. All of the parents felt that parents/adults should play with their children as well as observe them playing. The main reason given was to provide emotional support for their children. Other reasons included promoting an understanding of their children, moulding their behaviour and boosting their self-confidence. Following a pilot study within Tower Hamlet's Educational Psychology Service, the authors approached training courses for EPs during 1997–98. EPiTs from the following universities took part:

1. Institute of Education. University of London
2. University College London
3. University of East London
4. Manchester University
5. Nottingham University.

Some practising psychologists also volunteered to participate in the research to refine the PBA model. These volunteer EPiTs and practising EPs yielded data on a national level. The use of the PBA model in assessing a young child followed by the completion of a questionnaire was the recommended research method. It was suggested that the EPiTs could apply this model on their course placements in various Educational Psychology Services and practising EPs could use the model in their day-to-day work. In order to challenge PBA's effectiveness, two broad themes were explored through research questions specifically focusing on the user-friendliness and usefulness of its application.

The overall response was positive. The outcome of the research resulted in changes to the original PBA schedule. The following amendments were made:

- The front sheet was devised.
- The guidelines were refined.
- The wording of the scaling was changed.
- The comment section was elaborated upon including the concept of 'unscorable'.

In the PBA Prompt-Sheet:

- omissions, additions and changes were made to the descriptors
- the grid format was changed to enhance clarity
- minor changes to the Participatory Play Section were made
- the assessment summary sheet was devised.

Overall, this study made a significant impact on the assessment format but further research may be necessary to enhance its quality and application.


## PBA model

The authors' PBA (Figure 6.1) is an approach which combines observation and adult participation in determining a child's strengths and weaknesses.

### PBA = Observation + Participatory Play.

As an assessment tool it is accessible to both parents and professionals in a range of contexts. PBA enables adults to conduct assessments through the child's familiar play situation. Due to controversy surrounding norm-referenced assessment on cultural and linguistic grounds, a criterion-referenced approach has been considered more acceptable. On the one hand, norm-reference testing focuses on task performance whereas criterion-based assessment explores the context of learning potential and features that might empower the child to cope more successfully (Newson 1993).


## The aims of PBA

PBA enables adults to conduct an assessment through the child's familiar play situation. This model aims to provide knowledge and understanding of the child which adults can use to take the child's play/learning forward. This process should support communication between significant adults and may lead to changes in the child's play/learning environment. PBA consists of two phases: Observation and Participatory Play.

## Play-Based Assessment (PBA)

### The authors' PBA schedule contains:

- Background Information Sheet
- PBA Guidelines (Observation)
- PBA Prompt Sheet
- PBA Guidelines (Participatory Play)
- Assessment Summary Sheet

## Background Information Sheet

| | |
|---|---|
| Name of Child: | Date of birth: |
| Address: | Ethnicity: |
| Name of school/nursery/other: | First language: |
| Nature of child's difficulties: | |

| |
|---|
| Additional information: |
| Dates of assessment: |
| Duration:            Location: |
| Adult present: |

**Figure 6.1** Authors' PBA

## PBA Guidlines, observation phase

In PBA observation is an essential part of the assessment format because it provides useful insight into a child's understanding, learning pattern and learning potential. The assessor should allocate a minimum of 90 minutes to carry out a thorough PBA. This could be spread across two sessions within a four-week period. As part of PBA the suggested observation schedule highlights five main areas of a child's development (see Figure 6.2). The scale from 1–3 refers to a continuum of ability in the areas of Physical, Language, Cognitive (Thinking and Learning), Social and Emotional Development. Each child's skills are interrelated and reflect social and cultural factors. During the period of observation this profile can be used as a prompt and record sheet for the assessor when observing the child in solitary or group play or both. In order to use this profile most effectively the assessor may focus on each area of the child's development separately to ensure adequate details are obtained.

This basic schedule is *scaled* as follows:

Undeveloped:   1

Developing:     2

Developed:      3

These scores obtained could be used to compare the child's current level of functioning rather than comparing him/her to other children of the same age. In other words PBA is a criterion- rather than a norm-referenced form of assessment. The profile obtained can be used to highlight areas of development and/or discrete skills as strengths and will indicate the need for further investigation or immediate intervention. For example a score of **1** would indicate significant difficulty, **2** would suggest potential for improvement and **3** developed skills and consistent progress in this area. **Others** refers to any additional skills/behaviour observed by the assessor. The **Comments** section may be used to:

- highlight queries regarding scores
- give reasons known for high/low scores
- provide examples
- anticipate child's learning potential in discrete areas and the scope for mediation
- note 'unscorables' such as alertness, responsiveness and interest.

The **Assessment Summary Sheet** should highlight the child's strengths and weaknesses in relation to his/her general areas of development. Strengths constitute mainly **2s** and **3s** and weaknesses mainly **1s**. Action may need to be taken in relation to the development of the child's discrete skills and his/her approaches to learning through appropriate mediation.

# PBA Prompt Sheet

| Areas of development | Solitary | 1 | 2 | 3 | Group | 1 | 2 | 3 |
|---|---|---|---|---|---|---|---|---|
| **Physical** | Strength | | | | Strength | | | |
| | Mobility | | | | Mobility | | | |
| | Balance/posture | | | | Balance/posture | | | |
| | Whole body coordination | | | | Whole body coordination | | | |
| | Ball skills | | | | Ball skills | | | |
| | Spatial awareness | | | | Spatial awareness | | | |
| | Hand–eye coordination | | | | Hand–eye coordination | | | |
| | Manipulation | | | | Manipulation | | | |
| | **Others:** | | | | **Others:** | | | |
| **Language** | Imitation | | | | Imitation | | | |
| | Gesture/pointing | | | | Gesture/Pointing | | | |
| | Eye contact | | | | Eye contact | | | |
| | Listening (appropriate response) | | | | Listening (appropriate response) | | | |
| | Duration of on-task behaviour | | | | Duration of on-task behaviour | | | |
| | Vocalisations | | | | Vocalisations | | | |
| | Babbling | | | | Babbling | | | |
| | Naming (single words) | | | | Naming (single words) | | | |
| | Short phrases (2/3 words) | | | | Short phrases (2/3 words) | | | |
| | Sentences | | | | Sentences | | | |
| | Syntax | | | | Syntax | | | |
| | Pronunciation | | | | Pronunciation | | | |
| | Vocabulary | | | | Vocabulary | | | |
| | Following instructions | | | | Following instructions | | | |
| | Pre-reading skills | | | | | | | |
| | | | | | **Plus:** | | | |
| | | | | | Turn taking/sharing (non-verbal) | | | |
| | | | | | Turn taking/sharing (verbal) | | | |
| | | | | | Role-play | | | |
| | | | | | Communication (non-verbal) | | | |
| | | | | | Communication (verbal) | | | |
| | | | | | Seeking attention | | | |
| | | | | | Following instructions | | | |
| | **Others:** | | | | **Others:** | | | |

**Figure 6.2** (continued overleaf)

# PBA Prompt Sheet

| Areas of development | Solitary | 1 | 2 | 3 | Group | 1 | 2 | 3 |
|---|---|---|---|---|---|---|---|---|
| **Cognitive** | Sorting (colour, shape, size) | | | | Sorting (colour, shape, size) | | | |
| | Matching (colour, shape, size) | | | | Matching (colour, shape, size) | | | |
| | Sequencing (colour, shape, size) | | | | Sequencing (colour, shape, size) | | | |
| | Number concept | | | | Number concept | | | |
| | Logical thinking | | | | Logical thinking | | | |
| | Memory skills | | | | Memory skills | | | |
| | Ability to pretend (role-play) | | | | Ability to pretend (role-play) | | | |
| | | | | | **Plus:** | | | |
| | | | | | Group problem-solving | | | |
| | **Others:** | | | | **Others:** | | | |
| **Social** | | | | | Sharing | | | |
| | | | | | Turn taking | | | |
| | | | | | Imitating | | | |
| | | | | | Gesturing | | | |
| | | | | | Initiating contact | | | |
| | | | | | Leading | | | |
| | | | | | Being led in group | | | |
| | | | | | Accepting peer/adult interaction | | | |
| | | | | | **Others:** | | | |
| **Emotional** | Occupying oneself | | | | Sharing | | | |
| | Smiling | | | | Smiling | | | |
| | Laughing | | | | Laughing | | | |
| | Crying | | | | Cooperating | | | |
| | Controlling him/herself | | | | Controlling him/herself | | | |
| | Responding to change | | | | Responding to change | | | |
| | **Others:** | | | | **Others:** | | | |
| **Comments** | | | | | | | | |

**Figure 6.2**

## PBA Guidelines, Participatory Play phase

The second component of PBA is Participatory Play where the assessor interacts with the child in a play situation individually or as part of a group. This phase of the assessment complements the earlier observation and provides a fuller picture of the child. Behaviours that were evident from observation can be explored further through Participatory Play. The adult is directly and equally involved in the child's play. In worthwhile Participatory Play the assessor needs to consider the following points in three essential stages:

Stage I: Pre-play
Stage II: Play
Stage III: Post-play

### *Stage I: Pre-play (preparation for assessment)*

- Be specific about the information you will be gathering (refer to PBA Prompt Sheet if necessary).
- Decide the number of sessions.
- Negotiate timing and type of activities with other adults as far as possible.
- Decide the duration and the time.
- Decide location.
- Consider the cultural/linguistic factors.
- Familiarise yourself with the child and his/her environment.
- Decide mode of communication.
- Decide the role of other adults.
- Decide on group or individual play focus.

### *Stage II: Play (adult–child interaction, individually or as part of a group)*

- Consider proximity to child.
- Allow child to initiate as far as possible.
- Participate at the child's level.
- Guide/lead when necessary.
- Share agenda.
- Be aware of child's basic needs.
- Ensure flexibility in approach and ease of communication.
- Initiate and support pleasurable and positive interaction.

### *Stage III: Post-play (completion of assessment)*

- Phase out gradually.
- Record and structure information gathered by completing the PBA Prompt Sheet.

- Structure information gathered (refer to available standardised checklists if age-norms are needed).
- Feed back to other adults.
- Plan next step.

**Assessment Summary Sheet**

| |
|---|
| Child's name:                                    Date of birth: |
| Name of school/nursery/other: |
| Strengths identified through PBA: |
| Areas to target/develop: |
| Action: |
| Immediate: |
| Future: |
| Assessment completed by: |
| Name: |
| Title: |
| Date: |

## Conclusion

PBA has similarities with other assessment schedules and checklists but it has distinctive characteristics. It is:

- criterion-referenced
- context-embedded
- spontaneous
- accessible
- self-reinforcing
- culture-friendly
- suitable for all ages and ranges of ability.

Other important aspects of PBA are:

- its scope for assessment over time
- a means for achieving a full picture of child
- a curriculum planning/monitoring strategy
- an approach which focuses on the child's rather than the adult's agenda
- an approach which has potential for use dynamically
- an approach with scope for mediation, as assessment and intervention are taking place side by side.

The central feature of this model of assessment is the interaction of the child and adult through the medium of play. The child takes the lead while the adult observes or participates without affecting the pace or flow of the play. While interacting with the child, the adult acts as a 'go-between' between the child and his/her learning experiences. His learning is assisted though the adult's awareness of what the child needs to learn and how the adult acts upon it. This is also known as mediation and will be further discussed in relation to the work of Vygotsky and Feuerstein in Chapters 7 and 8.

*Note:* A separate PBA assessment schedule (unpublished copy) can be requested from the authors as commercial publication is currently under consideration.

*Chapter 7*

# Mediated learning experiences and play

## Thinking, learning and play – definitions and links

Throughout this book the authors have supported an interactionist approach to play. In this chapter relevant theories are explored in terms of their significance to play and how play can provide a medium for thinking and learning as a child grows and develops.

To begin with, it is important that the concepts of play, thinking and learning are differentiated and the links between them are understood. Play is defined:

> in terms of its overt and assumed characteristics. A child's play is elicited in response to a person/object in a context where he/she feels secure. Over time the child expends physical and mental energy for pleasure through the application of skills such as improvisation and creativity. As a state, play assumes absorption, concentration and an escape to a world that the child creates for him or herself individually or as part of a group.
>
> (Sayeed and Guerin 1997 p. 46).

While playing the child is engaged physically and emotionally and absorbed in his/her thoughts.

Thinking refers to the acquisition, storage and use of knowledge and skills. Through the thinking process a child learns the meaning of the world around him/her, makes sense of it and uses it. As a child grows and develops, physical, psychological and social changes usually occur in sequence. Learning is the process by which the child's development is modified by experience. When a child is developing normally his/her learning should progress; conversely, when a child's development is delayed or disordered due to within-child or environmental factors, his/her learning is affected. In the case of young children play is a natural and universal medium for thinking, learning and developing. The context for play (including opportunities for adult interaction) can either help or hinder the capacity of the child to learn through play.

Vygotskian psychology explores the nature of development, learning, language, thought, concept formation and children's play. His theory offers scope to interpret play in terms of thinking and learning.

## Vygotsky's sociocultural theory

Vygotsky (1978) viewed learning and development in childhood as a multidimensional, complicated process. He understood child development in terms of shifts in the child's thinking. Unlike Piaget (1964), who advocated a structured sequence of stages in the child's development, where development is led by learning, Vygotsky emphasised that learning is led by development and can be enhanced through social interaction. Vygotsky did not view the child's cognitive development in isolation but gave consideration to his/her social, cultural and historical background. He emphasised that a child's higher level learning could be achieved through an interaction with a more experienced peer or adult through the process of 'internalisation'.

The process of internalisation is gradual and occurs at two levels:

1. Social: The shift in the child's learning as a result of help from an adult.
2. Psychological: The child takes more initiative with adult guidance until gradually he/she becomes more independent in regulating the learning process for him/herself and controlling what and how he/she learns.

Though this view of thinking and learning may appear complicated it can often be observed in practice. For example, when a child does not know how to solve a jig-saw puzzle his/her parents or another adult may break the activity into steps and draw the child's attention to specific features, e.g. colours and shapes. As the child learns to do the puzzle, the parents/adult may gradually withdraw support, encourage the child to complete the puzzle independently and move from regulation by others to self-regulation.

The role of adults and how they communicate is fundamental to how children learn. Central to the interaction between the child and adult is the use of language, described by Vygotsky as an essential 'psychological tool'. The adult's language must be adapted to the child's level of learning and development, it must match the child's progress and form part of a 'scaffold' for new learning to take place.

In the fields of educational and child psychology the most widely valued and used concept suggested by Vygotsky is the Zone of Proximal Development (ZPD). The Zone of Proximal Development can be defined as the difference between a child's *actual developmental level as determined by independent problem-solving' and the higher level of 'potential development as determined through problem-solving under adult guidance or in collaboration with more capable peers'* (Vygotsky 1978 p. 86 – orginal in italics). The ZPD defines those functions that have not yet matured but are in the process of maturation, the functions that will mature tomorrow but are currently in an embryonic state. These functions could be termed the 'buds' or 'flowers' of development rather than the 'fruits' of development.

In summary he maintained that:

- Everyone functions at less than their full capacity.
- It is possible to estimate potential for learning.
- Important cognitive acquisition occurs in the context of social interaction.

The adult helps the child to achieve actions that the child will later achieve independently.

> The word 'proximal' (or nearby) indicates that the assistance provided goes just slightly beyond the child's current competence, complementing and building on the child's existing abilities instead of directly teaching the child new behaviour. (Cole and Cole 1996 p. 211)

The ZPD is important in order to determine the child's current level of functioning but also how the adult can lead the child on ahead of his/her development. In addition to the child's actual level of functioning it identifies his/her potential. This should indicate the amount, level and kind of support the child needs and facilitate planning around the child's needs for the adult. Following some research, Resing (1997 p. 71) suggested that 'the degree of help needed to reach an independent solution of the task can be seen as an indication of the inverse of the width of the child's zone of proximal development'. In other words the more help that a child needs the less is his/her learning potential. The Graduated Prompt method by Campione and Brown (1987) can be used as an indicator of a child's ZPD. For example, if under identical conditions (same age, ability and background), Child A needs considerably more prompting than Child B to complete the same task then the learning potential of Child A is less than Child B. Other procedures such as Learntest (Guthke and Wingerfeld 1992) have been formulated to raise the achievement of children by repetition, prompts and systematic feedback during the test or an extended training programme between two testing situations (pre-test and post-test).

Brown and Ferrara (1985) argued that the assessment of ZPD should include task analysis and the transfer of learning. The idea of breaking tasks into smaller steps and generalising learning from one task to another coincides with theories of learning and behavioural psychology.

Cognitive theorists have emphasised the value of metacognition which is an understanding of one's own thinking processes that underpin the ability to problem-solve. Metacognitive approaches such as those of De Bono's Cognitive Research Trust (CORT) (1973) and Ashman and Conway's Process Based Instruction (1993) emphasise that children need to be explicitly taught a range of thinking strategies which they can subsequently use in order to become expert problem-solvers. Metacognitive strategies taught by an adult may move a child from his/her actual level of development to his/her potential.

A static form of assessment, such as a psychometric measure, yields only a 'snapshot' of what the child can do at a particular time but does not give the assessor any information about the child's approaches to learning. Dissatisfaction with these forms of assessment have led to the development of Dynamic Assessment, the underlying characteristics of which are:

1. The assessor actively works to facilitate learning and induce active participation in the learner.

2. The assessment focuses on process rather than product – in this case the process of metacognition.

3. The assessment produces information about learner modifiability and the means by which the change is best accomplished.

(Lidz 1991)

In other words, through interaction the adult actively encourages the child to participate in his/her own learning during the assessment session. Particular attention is paid to how the child learns (strategies) rather than what he/she learns (content/task). The assessment procedure aims to gather information about the learner's potential to become a more effective learner and how this can happen.

In recent years Dynamic Assessment tools such as the Learning Potential Assessment Device (LPAD) were developed by Feuerstein *et al.* (1983) to establish children's learning potential as opposed to the child's learning ability:

... a method for assessing the potential of children, adolescents and adults for growth in specific cognitive processes, first by guided exposure to problems and processes of thought and subsequently by their own individual efforts.

(Feuerstein *et al.* 1983)

In the case of young children, David Tzuriel (1997) developed Dynamic Assessment tests and methods based on Vygotsky's and Feuerstein's theories. He described how approaches for pre-school children differ from other Dynamic Assessment approaches:

• The assessment materials and procedures must be developmentally appropriate for young children, e.g. game-like activities.

• The adult must provide gradual opportunities for bridging between concrete and abstract thinking. Advances in the child's thinking in the assessment situation may not be maintained in unsupported learning situations.

• The adult must adapt his/her communication style to suit the young child, e.g. awareness of own voice and gesture, in response to the child's psychological state and readiness to learn.

Tzuriel has developed Dynamic Assessment for two purposes: clinical/educational for gathering qualitative data, and measurement/research to collect quantitative data, either of which can be used with young children, depending on the purpose of assessment. A baseline phase is incorporated into his tests for young children to identify their existing cognitive skills before the actual test is administered. He uses two scoring methods – 'partial credit' and 'none-or-all' to identify small-scale improvements and to give young children a better chance to succeed. Specific attention is paid to the transfer of learning, facilitated and measured by some of his tests such as Children's Inferential Thinking Modifiability (CITM) and Cognitive Modifiability Battery (CMB). He believes that mediation should address the child's level of learning as well as the differentiation of materials used. While being assessed, the child's emotional and motivational states need to be taken into consideration, including lack of confidence and fear of failure. Throughout the assessment, the assessor must be creative in deciding about which test items should be used on basis of the test principles.

## Vygotsky's view of play

Vygotsky did not specifically develop a theory of play, but his social constructivist theory offers a perspective on play which focuses mainly on imaginary play and its function as a basis for development in pre-school years. His views have been subject to differential interpretations in an attempt to link play, learning and development. Four aspects of Vygotsky's theory can be elaborated in the context of play.

### *The social origin of play and its link with the emotional development of the child*

Vygotsky emphasised that in the play situation the child's interaction with the environment is satisfying and rewarding. Consequently he/she is motivated to continue to play, fulfilling his/her emotional needs. Play can be maintained in social and solitary play situations if the child feels satisfied, motivated and rewarded. This can be presented as shown in Figure 7.1.

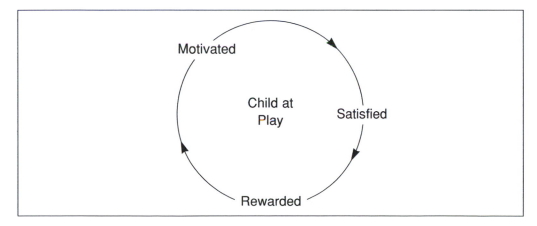

**Figure 7.1** The maintenance of play

In the context of play, rules are created and adapted by the player(s). Paradoxically, rules of the imagination both free the child from the constraints of the nursery or home where he/she is playing and, at the same time, can introduce order in the imaginary world created by the child. The following example helps to illustrate this point:

*Salim was seated on a wooden block wearing a black hat.*

*Salim:     I'm the fireman. I'm going out to water the fire.*
*Teacher:  No you can't go out it's nearly lunchtime.*

*Salim pauses for 10 seconds. He pulls a chair near to the wooden block and sits on it, gesturing as if to drive.*
*Taslima approaches Salim.*

*Taslima:  What are you playing?*
*Salim:     I'm the fireman. I'm driving the fire engine and I'm watering the fire*
*                (gestures a spraying action).*
*Taslima:  Are you coming for lunch?*
*Salim:     Yes, I'm a hungry fireman.*
*Teacher:  You will wet the table if you don't put away the hose!*

Constraints of the environment, e.g. an adult-directed nursery or home setting, will have implications for the child's approach to play. Given the social setting, adult rules may conflict with child's rules in the play context. As we know adult's rules are generally in the real world whereas the child's rules oscillate between the real world and his/her imaginary world. In the above example Salim was grappling with the expectations of the real world (as identified by his teacher) but managed to reach a compromise, enabling him to play imaginatively.

### Play, cognition and learning

> In play the child functions above his (her) average age, above his (her) everyday behaviour; in play he (she) is head high above his (her) self.
>
>                                                    (Butterworth and Harris 1994 p. 23)

While playing, the child learns through either 'direct exposure' to play activities or 'mediation'. Direct exposure is when a child learns incidentally and without the support of others. Children can learn through direct exposure when the play activities are conducive to the needs of the individual child or group of children. Adult facilitation or mediation is necessary when the child is not playing at his/her potential. Play provides context to determine the child's ZPD while the adult scaffolds his/her learning experience supporting the development of thinking skills. While playing, movement between reality and the imaginary world of a child leads to higher level thinking.  In the previous example of Salim in the role of a fireman, when reality (lunchtime) was imposed on him he used his higher level thinking to combine fantasy and reality in order to conserve and maintain his play.

## The imaginary element of play

Vygotsky attaches significance to imaginary as opposed to other types of children's play. In his opinion, during imaginary play the child is absorbed in his/her own creativity which leads to the development of abstract thinking. The child creates rules where they do not exist in reality and suspends rules through the imagination. From an observer's standpoint it is difficult to make sense of the process taking place when the child is totally absorbed in his play. This has led to controversy among play providers who have difficulty evaluating the process of imaginative play. Some play providers struggle to attach importance to this kind of play and tend to criticise its idealisation in search of a tangible outcome (behaviour) which can be observed.

## The importance of language in play

Language is central to the play and learning process. Vygotsky described language as 'a psychological tool' for thinking and learning for children at an early stage of language development or those with language delay; gesture, as opposed to verbal language, is a likely 'tool of play'. Where a child's play is being supported by an adult the latter may need to adapt his/her language to suit the child's needs and facilitate progress. In the case of Salim his teacher supports his role as a fireman by using complementary vocabulary such as 'wet' and 'hose'.

## Feuerstein's theories

Vygotskian psychology has been interpreted in a range of ways by professionals and academics in the field of education and social science. With colleagues, Feuerstein developed theories based on Vygotsky's ZPD. Feuerstein believed that individuals have the capacity to change their cognitive functions through adapting the processes of perception, thinking, learning and problem-solving in order to cope with changes and challenges in everyday life. His theories have significant implications for understanding individual differences and SEN as they highlight the importance of learning potential over performance. Feuerstein's approaches are based on his theories of Structural Cognitive Modifiability and Mediated Learning Experience.

### Structural Cognitive Modifiability (SCM)

Feuerstein believes that a person's thinking and learning can change irrespective of age, cause and severity of difficulty. Cognitive modifiability means that a person's cognitive functions can be changed and developed. Three main characteristics of SCM are:

- permanence – cognitive changes are durable and can last over time;
- pervasiveness – when change takes place in one part of a person's cognition it affects the whole;
- centrality – changes in a person's cognition are continuous and self-regulating.

This idea can be better understood with reference to Burden (1987) who describes human beings as open systems, subject to change throughout their lives, regardless of their age, kind or severity of their disabilities.

As explained earlier, there are two main ways in which children learn. These include incidental learning or learning through the support of more skilled others. Incidental learning or 'direct exposure' is more likely to be random and unsystematic, which may result in poor learning habits and related consequences for the child's overall achievements. SCM needs to be understood in the context of Mediated Learning Experience Theory.

## *Mediated Learning Experience (MLE)*

MLE is the process by which an adult (parent, teacher, etc.) or more able peer and child interact in relation to an activity. In accordance with the child's needs the adult adapts the frequency, order, intensity of the activity and the context where it takes place. The adult (mediator) arouses care, curiosity and alertness in the child so that the child understands the characteristics of the activity in order to perform the task successfully.

The following key points need to be taken into account in order to understand MLE:

- The amount, quality, intensity, frequency and duration of what is needed for adequate cognitive development will vary according to the individual needs of the child and the level and appropriateness of the task.
- Approach to tasks, attitude, motivation and emotional state can affect the child's perception, thinking, learning and problem-solving skills.
- If children are denied access to, or have inadequate access to, mediated learning their social and academic learning is affected.
- Factors which are known to affect learning such as poverty, learning difficulties, parental education and emotional needs can be offset by MLE.
- MLE can take place in all cultures and ways of thinking within cultures are transmitted through MLE. Feuerstein's Syndrome of Cultural Deprivation refers to children who do not have the experience of mediated learning from their parents, grandparents and older siblings.
- Learning opportunities that may have been missed by parents can be mediated by teachers or other adults at a later stage.

In describing a mediational teaching style, Haywood (1993) emphasised some of the above points. It is generally accepted that environmental and natural variables affect a child's learning and subsequent performance. Feuerstein believed that these variables exist and the extent to which they affect the child's learning ability and performance is contingent upon the quality of the MLE.

According to David Tzuriel:

> MLE interactions were conceived by Feuerstein as a proximal factor that explains individual differences in learning and cognitive modifiability. Factors such as organic deficit, poverty, socioeconomic status and emotional disturbances, might correlate with learning ability, but they affect learning ability only through the proximal factor of MLE.
>
> (Tzuriel 1997. Pre-publication copy, 'Learning and Instruction' provided during a Training Course on DA in Binoh Centre, London)

What happens during an MLE? According to Arbitman-Smith *et al.* (1984),

> Mediating the learning experiences of children...includes but is not limited to, such functions as stimulus selection (helping children to reduce the number and complexity of available stimuli by attending selectively), focusing on relevant aspects of a stimulus complex, repeating exposure to important stimuli, perceiving and understanding similarities and differences, sequential relationships, dimensionality, antecedents and consequences, commonalities in experience, and such operations as comparing, categorising, relating past present and future and grasping the concept of generalisability of experience to new situations.            (In Haywood 1993 p. 31)

During mediation the interactive process between the child and adult is a complex one which can include the examples of roles, actions and processing in Table 7.1.

**Table 7.1** Examples of how a child learns and an adult mediates

| Child | Adult |
| --- | --- |
| Selects an activity | Helps child to select activity and reduce its complexity |
| Focuses on relevant aspects | Exposes child to the activity repeatedly |
| Perceives and understands similarities and differences | Reinforces |
| Transfers learning principle to new situation | 'Bridges' by connecting child's past and present and future experiences |

## Mechanisms for MLE

The most fundamental and commonly used strategies applied in the mediated teaching and learning situation are:

- *Process questioning.* The adult asks 'how?' questions and encourages the child to think about the strategies that he/she needs to use before solving the problem. The child finds out for himself/herself what to do first and how he can find out what to do next. Self-questioning supports the development of metacognitive skills which the child can apply in a range of contexts.
- *Bridging.* This refers to the process where different applications of a thinking process or strategy are discussed between the child and adult. The adult helps the child to elicit the principle from experience and asks the child how the principle could be applied in a different situation. Both content and the 'cognitive function' of the child can be bridged.
- *Teaching about rules.* Through questioning and discussion between the child and mediator rules are elicited in relation to problems. They are applicable in future similar situations. Rule-making and application is the essence of generalisability.
- *Challenging and requiring justification.* The mediator challenges all answers given by the child – correct or incorrect. This helps the child to reflect on the learning process and solution to the problem. This allows the child to be critical of his/her strategies and maintains his/her attention.
- *Emphasising order, predictability, systems, sequence and strategies.* It can be assumed that the world has a natural order. In the mediated learning situation the adult transmits this principle to the child such that the child can recognise order, systems and sequences within a given activity or problem and arrive at a desirable outcome.

### *Criteria for mediated learning*

The process of mediated learning refers not only to *how* the adult mediates (mechanisms used) but also *what* the adult mediates. Feuerstein outlines a number of criteria for mediated learning as essential for successful mediation. The criteria are interrelated and overlapping in their meaning and application. For the purposes of this chapter, six of these criteria will be described and elaborated upon in terms of how they can apply to young children:

- *Intentionality and Reciprocity:* The learning intention is clear to the mediator and he/she ensures that the child is alert, attentive and ready to learn. The child responds to the interaction of the adults and consequently cognitive change takes place. This is reciprocated by the child helping him/her to feel at ease, confident and determined. With young children strategies such as repeatedly calling the child by name, using a range of auditory and visual stimuli and exaggerated use of voice and gesture can support the child's involvement and interest.

- *Mediation of Meaning:* When the mediator presents an activity this should be done with an emphasis on its meaning and significance, focusing the child's attention to the relevant features of the task. This concept has been well recognised in the field of teaching and learning (Ausubel 1968). Explanations are accompanied by enthusiasm and positive motivation. This can be done verbally or through non-verbal means such as voice intonation, gesture, repetition and modelling. 'Children who experience mediation of meaning will internalise this interaction and will later initiate attachment of meaning to new information rather than passively waiting for meaning to come.' (Tzuriel 1997)
- *Mediation of Trancendence:* An effective mediator reaches beyond the immediate situation and the needs of the child. He/she tries to attach a general principle that is not bound to the present. The mediator teaches strategies/rules which are applicable in other situations or at other times. With young children these principles can be practised by the presentation of toys or activities across a range of contexts which present similar challenges to his/her cognitive skills.
- *Mediation of Feeling of Competence:* The mediator plays an important role in building the child's confidence. The mediator can make the situation congenial to learning through providing opportunities for success and rewarding the learning process and product. When the learning of young children is being mediated the first task could be presented at a level well within the child's competence. The child should be praised for effort as well as achievement.
- *Mediation of Shared Participation:* Despite the different roles and positions the child and adult share the goal of the interaction equally. The interaction becomes two-way leading to structural cognitive change in the child. Practical activities for young children may include turn-taking and modelling by the adult.
- *Mediation for the Control of Behaviour:* A successful mediation exercise is contingent upon how the mediator regulates the child's behaviour. This may be done by reducing impulsivity and encouraging reflective behaviour. A calm approach helps the child to concentrate and process information accurately. This can be done by presenting the task in a manageable form, identifying the important components of the task and eliciting from the child what he/she is going to do and how. The child's undesirable learning behaviours, including a rushed approaches to tasks, should be discouraged and substituted with measured approaches. When mediating the learning of young children a step-by-step method can be introduced across a range of tasks with praise for following the task sequence.

During the mediational interaction the adult does not directly teach the task but rather the learning principle(s) so that the child can acquire these principles as part of his/her repertoire and apply them across a range of activities in different contexts. This approach to learning has particular benefits for younger children who are in the early stages of acquiring learning strategies which will mould their future learning. In the case of children with SEN who may struggle to acquire cognitive strategies through incidental learning experiences, MLEs are vital to ensure that they reach their individual learning potential.

The theories, concepts and principles discussed in this chapter will be elaborated and illustrated in the next chapter in the context of PBA and intervention.

*Chapter 8*

# Bridging the gap between assessment and intervention through play

## Assessment

In recent years the term 'assessment' has become familiar to people in all walks of life. Decisions in areas such as education, employment, personal finance and medicine, etc., are often made on the basis of an assessment of some kind. In the context of education this is geared towards National Curriculum attainment and linked to Local Education Authority resources. In the field of early years education increasing emphasis has been placed on assessment resulting in the development of baseline assessments, Desirable Learning Outcomes (DfEE 1966), Early Learning Goals (DfEE 1999) etc. This has implications for parental expectations around the success of their children and the provision made to support their children in meeting their educational targets.

Assessment in a conventional sense aims to identify a child's present level of functioning/development through observation and interaction with an adult in order to understand and plan to address the child's needs. Assessment takes place formally or informally using standardised or *ad hoc* measures at home or in an educational setting. The role of the assessor is no longer confined to the 'experts' and it is widely accepted that parents/carers and other significant adults in the life of the child can gather relevant information in order to support his/her learning and development.

For the majority of children assessment and education go hand in hand. Parents are the first adults in the role of assessors. This role gradually shifts to other adults such as carers and teachers beyond the child's home to the wider context. Parents/carers measure their children's progress through day-to-day quality interactions and observations. More and more parents are becoming active partners with professionals in assessment. The assessment process continues to broaden the adult's understanding of the child to enable the relevant adult to intervene appropriately. Models such as the Portage Early Education programme for children with SEN provides for a framework for parent–professional partnership in assessment and intervention. (White 1997)

In the field of education, assessment of children's learning by professionals has several forms. Assessment approaches range from informal observations to formalised norm-referenced testing. Trends in assessment methodology have been influenced by factors such as research, legislation, curriculum and information technology. When an individual child is being assessed, techniques should be carefully selected and be complementary to each other.

## *Approaches to assessment*

Amongst psychologists and other professionals, psychometric assessment has been used to provide objective, reliable and relevant information in relation to individual differences (intelligence, personality, language etc.). Statistical results inform the assessor of the extent to which a child's performance compares to that of his/her peers. This static form of assessment has a strong scientific underpinning in its development and is clinical in its administration (Trickey 1993).

There are some widely accepted drawbacks of using standardised tests, as these measures do not take into account factors such as the context of the assessment, the level of interaction with the assessor, the child's learning potential or suggestions for planning programmes.

In the UK during the 1980s a decline in the use of psychometric assessment in educational settings resulted in a shift towards a method of assessment that linked directly to the curriculum called Curriculum Related Assessment (CRA). CRA has its origin in principles of behavioural psychology where the child is assessed in relation to his/her performance across the curriculum. It is a formative method of assessment which allows the educator to make inferences about learning processes and adjust teaching methods, rate of teaching and contents of the curriculum. Task Analysis (breaking tasks into achievable steps) and Precision Teaching (explicit measure of teaching and learning in relation to identified tasks) were recommended as useful approaches.

Another assessment/teaching method called Direct Instruction recommended that the curriculum be expressed in the form of behavioural objectives, advocated selected teaching methods and consistent patterns of classroom organisation. CRA was considered to be a more acceptable form of assessment within the classroom context at that time as the 1981 Education Act paid particular attention to SEN and controversy surrounding culture-bias and over-emphasis on within-child factors in psychometric assessment. CRA allowed teachers to make effective informal assessments leading to classroom interventions but its suitability for bilingual learners was questioned due to the decontextualised nature of tasks (Cummins 1984). For example if a teacher was using task analysis to teach a skill to a bilingual learner there was scope for that skill to be taught separately to the curriculum offered in the classroom. Consequently it would become difficult for the learner to understand the relevance of his/her learning. Professionals such as educational psychologists who were at the forefront of assessing individual learning needs had difficulty implementing CRA due to legislative and ideological changes affecting how they worked (Ainscow and Tweddle 1988).

Assessment Through Teaching (ATT) was devised by Glaser (1982). In the 1980s, it was explored and used alongside CRA by professionals in education, including educational psychologists. ATT was designed to find out:

a)  what children learn in response to the curriculum on offer

b)  the quality of the classroom environment and

c)  the learning environment in the wider school.

It aimed to teach more efficiently those pupils with low attainment levels. ATT is a staged approach with particular emphasis on the learning context and explicit teaching with built-in feedback for teachers to modify their teaching methods. In its most simplistic form the following steps are taken by teachers in their role as assessors through teaching:

1. Determine the curriculum

2. Place the pupil on the curriculum

3. Decide what to teach

4. Organise the learning environment

5. Assess and evaluate the pupil's progress.

(Solity 1993)

As an approach to teaching and learning, ATT provides a useful framework for looking beyond the child to the task and learning environment. It recognises that many elements of the teaching process need to be modified in order to secure the learning of pupils, especially those with SEN. However its implementation requires environmental change in the classroom and often in the wider school context. Change on this scale may be beyond the scope of an individual professional using ATT.

During the 1990s there was a shift away from behavioural to cognitive psychology in an attempt to answer some of the 'why?' questions around children's learning (Frederickson *et al.* 1991). There was a shift towards the understanding that cognitive development forms the basis for all aspects of children's learning. This view raises more questions than answers and has implications for what the assessor needs to know and the skills the assessor needs to have.

There has been considerable interest in assessing what the child can do with the help of an assessor, that is, in identifying the child's potential rather than his/her ability on a given task in a specific context. Vygotsky's socio-cultural theory provided a foundation for the work of Feuerstein and others who developed Dynamic Assessment in the realm of children's learning (see Chapter 7).

At the core of Dynamic/Interactive Assessment are the social origins of cognitive development and the contrast between assisted and unassisted performance. The assessor is in the role of the learning partner, scrutinising the child's learning strategies rather than measuring his/her performance in relation to specific tasks. Dynamic/Interactive Assessment measures potential rather than performance. During the process of assessment the child's learning is mediated by the assessor. What the child can do with support of the mediator is an indicator of his/her potential for learning.

This Vygotskian concept is known as the Zone of Proximal Development (ZPD). 'What children can do with the assistance of others might be in some sense even more indicative of their mental development than what they can do alone' (Vygotsky 1978 p. 85).

The assessment aims to provide information about the child's learning ability that can be translated into strategies to support the child by the educator. The most significant features of Dynamic/Interactive approaches to assessment are:

• the mediating nature of the interaction between the child and the adult;
• the belief that thinking processes are modifiable, generalisable and durable.

The following set of assessor's questions should reveal the contrast between static and dynamic assessment:

**Table 8.1** Static vs Dynamic Assessment (Feuerstein *et al.* 1979)

| Static | Dynamic |
|---|---|
| What is the child's typical performance? | What is the child's maximum performance? |
| How much does the child know? | How can the child learn? |
| How well is the child likely to learn independently? | What teaching is needed to enable a child to learn at an acceptable level? |
| What areas of content have not been mastered? | What process deficiencies underlie previous learning failures and how can these be corrected? |

## Play and Dynamic Assessment

For young children, play is a desirable and integral part of every day life. For educators, assessment is an essential component of good practice. How can play and assessment come together? If other forms of assessment are introduced to the play setting or a play-based approach is applied to other kinds of assessment, can it work?

Standardised methods of assessment such as psychometrics have formal, inflexible procedures where spontaneous play does not fit, due to the neutrality of the adult and the restrictions placed on the child. CRA and ATT have the scope to be used by a range of professionals based in schools, not just visiting 'experts' from other agencies. Assessment focusing on the curriculum may have scope for play if:

- play is valued
- a play environment is provided
- children are encouraged to be autonomous, active and playful in their approach to learning
- the adult *intends* to use play to assess and plan in relation to the curriculum.

These conditions for play-related learning and assessment can be found in some early years and specialist settings where the curriculum is developmental. The previously-mentioned Portage Early Education Programme has excellent potential for *play* to be used by parents and Portage teachers/workers in assessing and teaching young children.

As mentioned in the previous chapter, Dynamic Assessment schedules such as Feuerstein's Learning Potential Assessment Device (LPAD) are used to assess older children's learning potential so there is limited scope for play. Tzuriel's contribution in the field of Dynamic Assessment for young children is substantial. His assessment tools for younger children can be used to approach tasks in a playful way but rigorous procedures such as face-to-face assessment and explicit expectations about the task to be completed do not have scope for playing freely and imaginatively in the assessment context. In the UK there has been limited progress in the development of Dynamic Assessment procedures for use with young children. The 'Bunny Bag' (Waters and Stringer 1997) was developed as a useful dynamic approach to assessment of pre-school children. This procedure is informed by developmental and cognitive theories such as those of Feuerstein and Vygotsky.

As mentioned in the previous chapter, the interactive nature of Dynamic Assessment makes this approach relevant to the play context. Dynamic Assessment is not a specific approach but a range of procedures. It incorporates mediated learning experiences, the child and adult engaging in a specific activity in an interactive way. The assessor needs to focus on:

- what is happening during the assessment (strategies used by the child);
- using mediation as an assessment/intervention strategy;
- the dynamic relationship between the child, the task and materials;
- the motivational and emotional aspects of the child's behaviour as part of the child's learning potential;
- the necessary conditions for intervention.

Assessment examines the child's cognitive deficiencies in relation to problem-solving in three phases, which Feuerstein and his colleagues call the Input Phase, the Elaboration Phase and the Output Phase. In brief, during the Input Phase the child gathers appropriate data to determine the nature of the problem. In the Elaboration Phase the child uses and understands the data made available to him/her. In the Output Phase the child communicates the solution.

In any conventional assessment, including most PBAs, assessment precedes intervention. In Dynamic Assessment the mediator is the key to intervention for the child. 'Making a difference' to the child is the focus of all interventions and while the child is being mediated, assessment and intervention are taking place simultaneously. The difference between conventional assessment and intervention and dynamic assessment are contrasted in Figures 8.1 and 8.2:

Assessment ➤ Intervention ➤ Assessment ➤ Intervention . . .

**Figure 8.1** Conventional assessment and intervention

| Assessment | | Assessment | | Assessment | |
|---|---|---|---|---|---|
| + | ➤ | + | ➤ | + | . . . . . . |
| Intervention | | Intervention | | Intervention | |

**Figure 8.2** Dynamic Assessment and intervention

Feuerstein's MLE principles can be effectively applied to most play situations where adults are interacting and assessing children with a view towards intervention. The authors' model of PBA has two components, Observation and Participatory Play. The Participatory Play element of the model has scope for the adult to assess through play and the child to learn through play. During PBA the adult's role

**Figure 8.3** Adult participation in child's play

shifts from one of observer to that of an assessor, participator and mediator.

The link between Dynamic Assessment and PBA in terms of their stages and processes are illustrated in Figure 8.4:

**Dynamic Assessment (DA)**

Child + Adult + Activity

Adult: Assess – Mediate (Stage 1)

**Play Based Assessment (PBA)**

Child Play

Adult: Assess through observation (Stage 1)

Child + Adult Play

Adult: Assess through participation (Stage 2)

Child + Adult Play

Adult: Assess and mediate through participation (Stage 3)

**Figure 8.4** Dynamic Assessment vs PBA

During Dynamic Assessment the adult assesses and mediates through interactions with the child in a single stage. In PBA the assessment takes place in three stages. In the first stage of PBA the adult gathers information through observing the child at play. In the second stage the adult participates in the child's play to complement information gathered through observation. By the end of the second stage the assessor will have a fuller picture of the child's functioning to plan for intervention. In the third stage the assessor not only participates in but also mediates the child's learning through play.

## Mediated Play Experience (MPE)

In Participatory Play the assessor's direct contact with the child enables an MLE to take place. Applying the principles, mechanisms and criteria of MLE in the Participatory Play situation the assessor should aim to bridge the gap between assessment and intervention. This process can be called a Mediated Play Experience (MPE). The following case examples illustrate how play can be a Mediated Play Experience and refer to Feuerstein's Criteria For Mediational Learning discussed in Chapter 7.

**Case Example 1: Group Mediated Play Experience.**

Ruzina, Tara and Tom walk in to the home corner in a school nursery.

Tara:     Let's play here.

Tom:     No, not good here.

Tara:     It's messy.

Tom:     I tell Miss.

Tom runs out of the home corner and approaches the teacher.

Ruzina:  Let's play a *Tidy Up Game*. I tidy the kitchen, I'm the Mummy. (Puts on a pair of 'Mummy' shoes).

Tara puts an apron on and picks up the dustpan and brush.

Tara:     I'm cleaning the floor, I'm Miss Bailey (nursery school cleaner).

Tom and teacher walk into the home corner.

Teacher: What game are you playing ?

Ruzina and Tara: *Tidy Up Game.*

Teacher: That sounds like a good game. Your house needs to be tidied up. Can I join in?

While the teacher observes, Tara starts to sweep the floor while objects are still lying on it. As Ruzina fills the cupboards haphazardly Tom takes out a pan and stands by the stove pretending to cook.

Tara:     We're not playing cooking. Miss can you tell him.

Teacher: What is the best way of playing this *Tidy Up Game?*

Ruzina:  Plates go in the plate cupboard and pans go in the pan cupboard.

Teacher: How do you know?

All three children are silent.

Teacher: Can you remember how you helped me to tidy the book corner?

Ruzina:  I know there are pictures on the cupboard.

She picks up a plate and puts it in the appropriate cupboard.

Tom:     I don't like this game.

Tom walks towards the door of the home corner.

Teacher: You are very good at playing in the home corner. You might like this new game.

Tom smiles and returns to the game.

Tom (to the teacher): I'm putting the small spoons in the small tray and you put the big spoons in the big tray.

Teacher: I'll be your partner.

She hands Tom more spoons lying around the kitchen.

Teacher: Good, we all know now what to do.

Tara:     This house will look nice and I'll be the Mum. Tom you can be the Dad.

Ruzina:  I like this game . . . Let's play *Tidy Up Game* tomorrow.

Teacher: Where else can we play this game ?

Tom:     In the huts . . . in the playground.

## *Analysis*

In the above play situation both the adult and children are engaged in a quality interaction where assessment and intervention took place simultaneously. Previous to the teacher's participation the children created their own agenda and identified a game they wanted to play. The teacher adopted the role of a sensitive mediator and player who encouraged the children to think more creatively and systematically through shared participation and without disrupting the flow of their game. Her style suggests an awareness of the children's play intention which she reciprocated through a shared agenda on equal terms. The teacher motivated the reluctant child, Tom, by emphasising his strengths and the novelty of the game. The children's feelings about their own competence as able players was communicated through her comments. Her calm approach allowed the game to flow smoothly reducing their impulsivity (as they wanted to play without a plan) and encouraging reflective behaviour. In accordance with Feuerstein's principle of Mediation of Transcendence, the teacher was able to encourage children to identify the use of their play strategies beyond the here and now (in the hut, playground, tomorrow).

The mechanisms employed by the teacher were similar to some of the characteristics of an MLE (Chapter 7). She used process questioning such as 'How do you know?' to encourage them to think about their own strategies and elicit rules. She referred to the children's past experience as well as identifying future benefits of the learned strategies. By so doing she 'bridged' thinking strategies between past, present and future. The teacher's mediation emphasised order and sequence thus the children were able to play successfully and predict the positive outcome of their play experience. Recognition of the pleasurable process and desirable product of this particular play was evident in the children's discussion when Ruzina said ' I like this game . . . let's play the Tidy Up Game tomorrow.'

**Case Example 2: Individual Mediated Play Experience.**

Samuel, aged four years, is in the family sitting room rummaging in his box of toys.

He quickly selects and returns toys to the box, seeming unsure about what he wants to play with. Samuel's father, Jason, is watching from the sofa. He walks towards him.

Samuel: Play with me, Dad.

He pulls him towards his toy box.

Jason:   What would you like to play ?
Samuel: I want the fruit puzzle.
Jason:   You enjoyed doing puzzles with your sister the other day.
Samuel: No, it was my teddy puzzle.

Both Samuel and Jason look in the box to find the board and puzzle pieces.

Jason:   How can we play ?

Samuel has already started to randomly squeeze the pieces into the board.

Jason:    Let's look at the pieces together first. You may know some of the
          fruit.
Samuel: Apple, banana, orange . . .

He picks up the pear piece.

Samuel: What is this one, Dad?
Jason:   You remember the fruit you ate with Mum.

Samuel pauses and jumps up.

Samuel: I know it's a pear.

Jason shows him the strawberry shape.

Jason:   What is this one called?
Samuel: Strawberry.
Jason:   Are you sure? How do you know?
Samuel: It's red. I like it in my grandma's house.
Jason:   Yes, you are right, ripe strawberries are always red. What will we
          do now?

Samuel gives him the banana shape.

Samuel: You put it in Dad.

Jason tries to fit it in the space for the apple.

Samuel: No, no it's not there . . . banana goes with banana.
Jason:   Good boy Samuel, now you know that all fruits have their own
          space. You can put them in.

Samuel perseveres and finishes the puzzle.

Samuel: Can I do Lily's (sister's) puzzle?

## *Analysis*

The interaction between Samuel and his father, Jason, was mediational in nature. In this participatory play situation Jason and Samuel were sharing the same agenda, trusting each other's contribution and valuing each other's role and responses. Jason nurtured his son's play through reducing Samuel's impulsivity when he was randomly squeezing the pieces on to the board. He supported his son's initiative and encouraged him to think in relation to the activity through process questioning and suggestions. He challenged and required justification of Samuel's knowledge of strawberries. He guided Samuel's learning by referring to his earlier experiences in different contexts, e.g. eating strawberries at his grandmother's house. They constructed simple rules, i.e. all ripe strawberries are red and each shape has a matching space on the puzzle. Jason enforced Samuel's confidence and rewarded his competence in this shared endeavour. This mediational play process should produce changes in Samuel's thinking that are generalisable and durable.

The nature of the adult's interaction with the child during play defines an MPE. The following examples of the adult's suggestions and responses aim to differentiate between a Non-MPE and MPE:

**Table 8.2** Questions and responses in MPE and Non-MPE

| Non-mediated Play Experience (Non-MPE) | Mediated Play Experience (MPE) |
| --- | --- |
| Let's play X . . . | How are we going to play? |
| Do you know that . . . ? | How did you know X . . . ? |
| Did you play X before? | Do you remember when you played X? (reference made to time, context, etc.) |
| What are you doing? | Why do you think you need to do X? |
| Well done | Well done for doing X |
| You have done X quickly | You have done X well by taking your time |
| What are you going to do? | What are we going to do together? |

A child and adult may share a play experience which may/may not be an MPE. The difference between an MPE and Non-MPE is based on the mediator's intention, expectation, approach and language, all of which are fundamental to the development of the child's thinking processes. The language of mediated play does not necessarily come naturally. In addition to some training it requires a conscious effort on the part of the mediator to use language that is easy enough for the young child to understand but appropriate to extend the child's thinking. The MPE needs to be carefully adapted and applied for children with SEN in general and in particular for children with language difficulties through non-verbal communication strategies.


## Conclusion

Questions have been raised about the suitability of Dynamic Assessment with young children as it was felt that, as pre-schoolers, they may be developmentally unable to access metacognitive processes. Lidz and Thomas (1987) found that children as young as three years have emerging cognitive processes. However Feuerstein's list of cognitive functions is not completely applicable to younger children and according to Mearig (1987), Dynamic Assessment for young children should 'emphasise the identification and strengthening of emergent cognitive functions instead of trying to correct deficiencies' (Waters and Stringer 1997).

The authors' PBA has evolved as a result of research and practice. It was initially based on developmental principles with a focus on identifying the child's strengths and weaknesses through observation. Practice suggested that if the adult participates in the child's play the information gathered through assessment is richer. The participatory element of the assessment led to the role of the adult being developed into that of a mediator. The concept of the authors' MPE was informed by theories of Vygotsky and Feuerstein.

# Chapter 9
# Final thoughts

As experienced practitioners working with young children and focusing on their learning and development, it was difficult to separate the players from their play. Observations in a number of settings highlighted the prevalence of play behaviour and play activities, suggesting that play is an integral part of children's lives. Children have an innate capacity to play in any given situation and as an enjoyable and fulfilling experience play seemed to offer unending scope for all children. Play settings were happy and absorbing environments where the vast majority of children participated without fear of failure. In many ways, these settings contrasted with learning environments for older children where success was based on task performance rather than opportunities to experiment with the real and the pretend. Such observations prompted the authors to explore the possibilities of play for understanding, assessing and supporting young children.

Adults have a generally-held view that play is an enjoyable experience for children but its value and status are not always widely acknowledged. This may be the case because children's play is taken for granted as their natural activity rather than as an activity that can be analysed and understood for the benefit of the child. Due to difficulties in relation to its definition, characteristics and the language used to typify play it has received criticism as well as praise. Two polarised viewpoints exist. Some forcefully advocate the social, educational and affective merits of play while others disregard childhood play as simply a means of passing time without any positive, observable outcome. Ideological conviction, resources and a legislative framework can give play the status it deserves. The International Association for the Child's Right to Play (IPA) has been lobbying to elevate the status of play by raising awareness, generating ideas and creating contexts for implementation of policies for play. The IPA (1977) declared: 'Children are the foundation of the world's future' and 'Play is a means of learning to live not a mere passing of time'.

In the UK there has been a steady flow of discourse and literature on the subject of children's play, emanating from practitioners and academics. Its educational value has been heightened through the relatively recent introduction of play-based curricula for pre-schoolers, indicating political approval and support at a national level. In local communities the activities on offer in playgroups, toy libraries and other early years settings would suggest that play is an obvious choice of activity. Across cultures, parents and carers have become understandably confused about what constitutes quality play as a result of the commercialism of the toy industry.

Play is inherently inclusive as every child can play, either alone or with others, with or without materials. The nature and sophistication of the child's play will depend on the child's individuality and the quality of the play environment. Play does not aim to 'normalise' children but rather supports their development as individuals among other children, 'able' or 'disabled'. Whereas factors such as social class, race, language and ability have the potential to divide children, play has the scope to unite them. Society as a whole should bear the responsibility of providing accessible and safe play opportunities for all children.

If adults accept that play has a key role in the learning and development of young children then play should be supported not only through material provision, but active involvement in the home, school and other settings. Professional play providers must acknowledge that parents have specific knowledge about their child and can play a central role in enhancing their child's learning through play. Where a shared acknowledgement of the importance of play develops, parents and professionals need to communicate and exchange ideas, experiences and preferences. Issues around how the child plays, what the child plays and what he/she plays with in the home and outside the home should be the focus of discourse. In collaboration, the adults should plan, support and celebrate his/her play and learning. As far as possible children themselves should be involved in this process. From an interactionist perspective the quality of involvement of the child and adult can make a significant difference to the child's functioning in all areas of his/her development. This has implications for the child's later learning in childhood, adolescence and adult life.

From the standpoint that play is valuable and useful for both the child and adults around him/her, the authors have attempted to understand play and use it for the purposes of assessment and intervention. Initially, play was considered in terms of observable behaviours while the child was playing. Later, this led to adult participation for the purposes of formulating a fuller picture of the child. Further exploration of theory and practice convinced the authors that the adult should not just participate in play but also mediate the child's learning. Although the authors' model of Play Based Assessment was developed on the basis of some research, further work is needed. This could include: refining the authors' model of PBA, evaluating the concept of an Individual Play Plan and exploring and extending the idea of simultaneous assessment and intervention through the Mediated Play Experience (MPE).

Global technological advancement and the rate of change will undoubtedly impact upon play in the future. This will have wide-ranging effects on society's view of play as reflected in the perception of adults. Inevitably it will change the way children play and learn as well as the materials/toys they use. The process of change will preserve and lose some of the conventional characteristics of play. On the positive side, play is likely to remain a multisensory experience and medium for learning. Challenges for parents and professionals may include children's preferences for playing with commercial, computerised play objects over 'natural' play materials. Early years play has generally facilitated the social and emotional development of the child through human interaction. Parents and professionals must guard against losing this vital element of play while appreciating and using the opportunities afforded to children during this technological era. As advocates of the interactionist perspective on play, the authors return to the ocean analogy for play, where scuba-diving must continue regardless of the increasing complexity of the ocean's conditions.

# Bibliography

Ablon, S. L (1996) 'The therapeutic action of play', *Journal of the American Academy of Child and Adolescent Psychiatry* **35** (4), 545–8.

Ainscow, M. and Tweddle, D. A. (1988) *Encouraging Classroom Success.* London: David Fulton Publishers.

Ainsworth, M., Blehar, M. C., Walters, E. and Wall, S. (1978) *Patterning Attachment: A Psychological Study of the Strange Situation.* Hillsdale, N.J: Lawrence Erlbaum Associates.

Allen, P. (1997) 'Social construction of self: Some Asian, Marxist and Feminist critiques of dominant Western views of self' in Allen, P. (ed.) *Culture and Self: Philosophical and Religious Perspectives East and West.* Westview Press.

Allesandri, S. M. (1991) 'Play and social behaviours in maltreated pre-schoolers', *Development and Psychopathology* **3**, 191–205.

Andreski, R. and Nicholls. S. (1993) *Establishing a Policy to Support Social Development.* London: Nursery World Publication.

Arbitman-Smith, R., Haywood, H. C. and Bransford, J. D. (1984) 'Assessing cognitive change', in Brooks, P., Serber, R. and McAuley, C. M. (eds) *Learning and Cognition in the Mentally Retarded.* New York: Erlbaum.

Ashman, A. F. and Conway, R. (1993) *Using Cognitive Methods in the Classroom.* London: Routledge.

Ausubel, D. (1968) *Educational Psychology. A Cognitive View.* New York: Guildford Press.

Bailey, D. and Wolery, M. (1989) *Assessing Infants and Pre-schoolers With Handicaps.* Columbus, OH: Merrill.

Bandura, A. (1977) *Social Learning Theory.* Englewood Cliffs, NJ: Prentice Hall.

Barrett, K. and Campos, J. J. (1987) 'Perspectives on emotional development: A functional approach to emotions', in Osofsky, J. (ed.) *Handbook of Infant Development*, 2nd edn. New York: Wiley.

Beardsley, G. and Harnett, P. (1998) *Exploring Play in the Primary Classroom.* London: David Fulton Publishers.

Bloch, M. and Adler, L. (1994) 'African children's play and the emergence of sexual division of labour', in Roopnarine, J., Johnson, J. and Hooper, F. (eds) *Children's Play in Diverse Cultures*. Albany, NY: State University of New York Press.

Bloch, M. and Pelligrini, A. (1989) *The Ecological Context of Children's Play*. New York: Ablex.

Bloom, B. (1964) *Stability and Characteristics in Human Change*. New York: John Wiley.

Bowlby, J. (1973) *Attachment and Loss: Separation*. New York: Basic Books.

Boxall, M. (1976) *The Nurture Group in the Primary School*. Inner London Education Authority.

Boyer, W. A. R. (1997) 'Playfulness enhancement through classroom intervention for the 21st century', *Childhood Education* **74**(2), 90–97.

Bremner, J. G. (1995) *Infancy*, 2nd edn. UK and USA: Blackwell.

Brewer, J. and Freud, S. (1985) *Studies on Hysteria. The Standard Edition of the Complete Psychological Works of Sigmund Freud*, Vol. 2. London: Hogarth Press.

British Psychological Society (1996) Report of a Working Party. *ADHD – A Psychological Response to an Evolving Concept*. London: BPS.

Brown, A. L. and Ferrara, R. (1985) 'Diagnosing Zones of Proximal Development', in Wertsch, J. V. (ed.) *Culture, Communication and Cognition: Vygotskian Perspectives*. New York: Cambridge University Press.

Bruce, T. (1991) *Time to Play in Early Childhood Education*. London: Hodder & Stoughton.

Bruner, J. S. (1972) 'The nature and uses of immaturity', *American Psychologist* **27**, 687–708.

Bruner J. (1996) *The Culture of Education*. Cambridge, Mass: Harvard University Press.

Burden, R. S. (1987) 'Feuerstein's instrumental enrichment programme: important issues in research and evaluation', *European Journal of Psychology of Education* **2**(1), 3–16.

Butterworth, G. and Harris, M. (1994) *Principles of Developmental Psychology*. Hove: Lawrence Erlbaum.

Campione, J. C. and Browne, A. L. (1987) 'Linking dynamic assessment with school achievement', in Lidz, C. (ed.) *Dynamic Assessment*, 82–115. New York: Guildford Press.

Carmichael, K. D. (1994) 'Play therapy for children with physical disabilities', *Journal of Rehabilitation* **60**(3), 51–4.

Christie, J. F. (1991) *Play and Early Years Development*. Albany, New York: State University of New York Press.

Christie, J. F. and Johnson, E. P. (1983) 'The role of play in social–intellectual development', *Child Development* **53**(1).

Claxton, G. (1984) *Live and Learn. An Introduction to the Psychology of Growth and Change in Everyday Life*. London: Harper & Row.

Cohn, D. (1991) 'Anatomically correct doll play of pre-schoolers referred for sexual abuse and those not referred', *Child Abuse and Neglect*, **15**, 455–66.

Cole, M. and Cole, R. (1996) *The Development of Children*, 3rd edn. New York: W. H. Freeman and Company.

Crowe, B. (1983) *Play is a Feeling*. London: George Allen and Unwin Publishers.

Cummins, J. (1984) *Bilingualism and Special Education: Issues in Assessment and Pedagogy*. Avon: Multilingual Matters.

Curtis, A. (1994) 'Play in different cultures and different childhoods', in Moyles, J. (ed.) *The Excellence of Play*. London: Open University Press.

Darwin, C. (1892) *The Expression of Emotions in Man and Animals*. Chicago: University of Chicago Press, 1975.

Davies, M. (1985) 'Beyond physical access for students with cerebral palsy?' *The Psychologist*, **8**(9), 401–4.

De Bono, E. (1973) *CORT Thinking*. New York: Pergamon Press.

Deardon, R. F. (1967) 'The concept of play', in Peters, R. S. (ed.) *The Concept of Education*. London: Routledge & Kegan Paul.

DES (1967) *The Plowden Report: Children and Their Primary Schools*. Central Advisory Council for Education England. London: HMSO.

DES (1978) *Special Educational Needs. The Warnock Report*. London: HMSO.

DES (1988) *Task Group on Assessment and Testing Report*. London: Department of Education and Science.

DES (1990) *Starting with Quality: Report of the Committee of Inquiry into the Quality of Educational Experiences Offered to 3 to 4 year olds. (Rumbold Report)*. London: HMSO.

DfE (1994) *Code of Practice on the Identification and Assessment of Special Educational Needs*. London: Department for Education.

DfEE (1996) *Desirable Outcomes of Children's Learning on Entering Compulsory Education*. London: SCAA.

DfEE (1997) *Excellence for All Children* (CM3785) Green Paper. London: HMSO.

DfEE (1999) *Early Learning Goals*. London: Qualifications Curriculum Authority.

Doyle, R. (1994) *Paddy Clarke, Ha, Ha, Ha*. London: Minerva Press.

Eichinger, J. and Wolman, S. (1993) 'Integration strategies for learners with severe multiple disabilities', *Teaching Exceptional Children* **26**(1), 18–21.

Erikson, E. (1963) *Childhood and Society*. London: Routledge & Kegan Paul.

Esposito, B. G. and Koorland, M. A. (1989) 'Play behaviour of hearing-impaired children. Integrated and segrated settings', *Exceptional Children* **55**, 412–19.

Farver, J. M., Kim, Y. K. and Lee, Y. (1995) 'Cultural differences in Korean and Anglo-American pre-schoolers' social interaction and play behaviours', *Child Development* **66**, 1088–99.

Faulkener, D. and Lewis, V. (1995) 'Intervention: Down's Syndrome and autism', in Bancroft, D. and Carr, R. (eds) *Influencing Children's Development*. Oxford: Blackwell Press.

Feitelson, D. (1977) 'Cross-cultural studies of representational play', in Tizard, B. and Harvey, D. (eds) *The Biology of Play*. London: Spastics International Medical Publications.

Feuerstein, R., Rand, Y. and Hoffman, M. (1979) *The Dynamic Assessment of Retarded Performers: The Learning Potential Assessment Device.* Baltimore: University Park Press.

Feuerstein, R., Haywood, H. C., Rand, Y., Hoffman, M. B. and Jensen, M. R. (1983) *Learning Potential Assessment Device (Manual).* Jerusalem: Hadassah – W/ZD Canada Research Institute.

Fiese, B. H. (1990) 'Playful relationships: A contextual analysis of mother– toddler interaction and symbolic play', *Child Development* **61**, 1648–56.

Fox, M. (1997) 'The multidisciplinary assessment of under fives with cerebral palsy' in Wolfendale, S. (ed.) *Meeting Special Needs in the Early Years.* London: David Fulton Publishers.

Fox, N. (1997) 'Attachment of kibbutz infants to mothers and metapelet' *Child Development* **48**, 1228–39.

Fredrickson, N. (1987) 'CRA: Has it had its day?', *Educational and Child Psychology* **10**(4), 14–26.

Fredrickson, N., Wright, A. and Webster, A. (1991) 'Psychological assessment: a change of emphasis', *Educational Psychology in Practice* **7**(1), 20–9.

Freud, S. (1922) *Beyond the Pleasure Principle.* Standard Edition. London: Hogarth Press.

Froebel, F. (1906) *The Education of Men.* New York: Appleton.

Garfinkel, H. (1967) *Studies in ethromethodology*, in Newton, C. (1988) '"Who knows me best?" Assessing pre-school children. Levels of participation in a child's world', *Educational Psychology in Practice* **3**(4), 35–9.

Garvey, C. (1991) *Play*, 2nd edn. London: Fontana Press.

Gaskins, S. and Goncu, A. (1992) 'Cultural Variation in Play: A Challenge to Piaget and Vygotsky.' (Quarterly) *Newsletter of the Laboratory of Comparative Human Cognition* **14**(3), 31–5.

Gaussen, T. H. (1984) 'The educational psychologist and the under twos: some problems and possibilities in infant assessment', *Journal of the Association of Educational Psychologists* **6**(2).

Glaser, R. (1982) *Teaching, Research and Education.* Pittsburg, PA: University of Pittsburgh Press.

Gleick, J. (1988) *Chaology.* London and New York: Heinemann.

Goldhaber, J. (1994) 'If we call it science then can we let the children play?', *Childhood Education* **71**(1), 24–8.

Griffiths, M. (1998). 'Fruit machine addiction: an issue for educational psychologists?', *Educational and Child Psychology* **15**(4), 33–44.

Groos, K. (1901) *The Play of Men.* London: William Heinemann.

Guthke, J. and Wingerfeld, S. (1992) 'The learning test concept. Origins, state of the art and trends', in Haywood, H. C. and Tzuriel, D. (eds) *Interactive Assessment*, 64–94. New York: Springer.

Hall, G. S. (1908) *Adolescence.* New York: Appleton.

Haste, H. (1987) 'Growing into rules', in Bruner, J. and Haste, H. (eds) *Making Sense: The Child's Construction of the World.* London: Methuen.

Haywood, C. (1993) 'A mediated teaching style', *Journal of Cognitive Education and Mediated Learning* **3**(1), 27–38.

Heino, F. L., Meyer-Bahlburg, D. A., Sandberg, E., Curtis, L., Dolezal, T. and Yager, J. (1994) 'Gender-related assessment of childhood play', *Journal of Abnormal Child Psychology* **2**(6), 643–61.

Hewes, J. C. (1987) 'Multiculturalism: Another dimension to play'. Report of the IPA World Conference, Stockholm.

Hodgkin, R. and Newell, P. (1998) *Implementation Handbook for the Convention on the Rights of the Child.* USA: United Nations Children's Fund (UNICEF)

Hoffman, L. W. (1991) 'The influences of the family environment on personality: acounting for sibling differences', *Psychological Bulletin* **110**, 187–203.

Hofstader, D. (1979) *Godel, Escher, Bach: An Eternal Golden Braid.* New York: Basic Books.

Howitt, D. and Owusu-Bempah, K. (1999) 'Education, psychology and the construction of black children', *Educational and Child Psychology* **16**(3), 17–29.

Hughes, B. (1990) 'Why is Play a Fundamental Right of the Child?' in *On Research and Study of Play.* Report of the IPA 11th World Conference. Tokyo, June 1990.

Hughes, F. (1994) *Childhood, Play and Development.* New York: Allyn and Bacon.

Hughes, M., Dote-Kwan, J. and Dolendo, J. (1998) 'A close look at the cognitive play of pre-schoolers with visual impairments in the home'. *Exceptional Children* **64**(4), 451–63.

Huizinga, J. (1949) *Homoludens. A Study of the Play Element in Culture.* London: Routledge & Kegan Paul.

Hutt, C. (1966) 'Exploration and Play in Children', *Symposia of the Zoological Society of London* **18**, 61–87.

IPA (1987) *Creativity through play.* Report of the 10th Conference of the International Association for the Child's Right to Play, IPA. Stockholm, IPA.

Isaacs, S. (1929) *The Nursery Years.* London: Routledge & Kegan Paul.

Isenberg, J. P. and Jacobs, J. E. (1982) *Playthings as Learning Tools. A Parent's Guide.* New York: John Wiley and Sons.

Izard, C. E (1978) 'On the ontagenesis of emotion and emotion–cognition relationships in infancy', in Lewis, M. and Rosenbloom, M. (eds) *The Development of Affect.* New York: Plenum.

Jacklin, C. N. and Maccoby, E. E. (1978) 'Social behaviour at thirty three months in same-sex and mixed-sex dyads', *Child Development* **49**, 557–69.

Jeffree, D. M., McConkey, R. and Hewson, S. (1979) *Let Me Play.* Hove: Lawrence Erlbaum.

Jenks, C. (1993) *Culture–Key Ideas.* New York and London: Routledge.

Johnson, J. F., Christie, J. F., and Yawkey, T. D. (1987) *Play and Early Childhood Development.* Glenview, IL: Scott, Foreman and Company.

Klugman, E. and Smilansky, S. (1990) *Children's Play and Learning: Perspectives and Policy Implications.* New York and London: Teachers' College Press and Columbia University.

Konner, M. (1975) 'Relations among infants and juveniles in comparative perspective', in Lewis, M. and Rosenblum, L. (eds) *Friendship and Peer Relations*, 99–129. New York: Wiley.

Konner, M. (1977) 'Evolution in human behaviour development', in Leidermann, P. H., Tulkin, S. and Rosenfield, A. (eds) *Culture and Infancy: Variations in Human Experience*. New York: Academic Press.

Laughlan, F. and Elliott, J. (1997) 'Using Dynamic Assessment materials as a tool for providing cognitive intervention to children with complex learning difficulties', *Educational and Child Psychology* **14**(4), 6–16.

Lehman, H. C and Witty, P. A. (1927) *The Psychology of Play Activities*. New Jersey: Bernes Cronberg.

Leslie, A. M. and Frith, U. (1990) 'Prospect for a cognitive neuropsychology of autism: Hobson's choice', *Psychological Review* **97**, 122–31.

Lewis, V. and Boucher, L. (1988) 'Spontaneous, instructed and elicited play in the relatively able autistic child', *British Journal of Developmental Psychology* **6**, 325–39.

Lidz, C. S. (1991) *Practitioner's Guide to Dynamic Assessment*. New York: Guildford Press.

Lidz, C. S. and Thomas, C. (1987) 'The pre-school assessment device: extension of a static approach', in Lidz, C. S. (ed.) *Dynamic Assessment: An Interactive Approach to Evaluating Learning Potential*. New York: Guildford Press.

Lindsey, E. W., Mize, J. and Gregory, S. P. (1997) 'Differential play patterns of mothers and fathers of sons and daughters: implications for children's gender role development', *Sex Roles: A Journal of Research* **37**(9–10), 643–62.

Mankodi, H. and Bhagia, D. (1990) 'Involvement of Kindergarten Children in Play Experiences'. *On Research and Study of Play*. Report of the IPA 11th World Conference. Tokyo, June 1990.

Manning, K. and Sharp, A. (1990) *Structuring Play in the Early Years at School*. Sussex, England: Ward Locke Educational in association with Drake Educational Associates.

Martin, C. L. and Little, J. K. (1990) 'The relation of gender understanding to children's sex-typed preferences and gender stereotypes', *Child Development* **61**, 1427–39.

Matterson, E. M. (1975) *Play With a Purpose For Under Sevens*. Harmondsworth: Penguin Books.

McConkey, R. (1985) 'Changing beliefs about play and handicapped children', *Early Child Development and Care* **19**, 79–94.

McCune, L. (1986) 'Play–language relationships. Implications for a theory of symbolic development', in Gottfried, A. W. and Brown, C. C. (eds) *Play Interaction. The Contribution of Play Material and Parental Involvement to Children's Development*. Lexington, MA: DC Heath.

McMillan, M. (1930) *The Nursery School*. London: Dent.

Mearig, J. S.(1987) 'Assessing the learning potential of kindergarten and primary-aged child', in Lidz, C. S. (ed.) *Dynamic Assessment: An Interactive Approach to Evaluating Learning Potential*. New York: Guildford Press.

Miller, S. (1968) *The Psychology of Play*. Penguin Books.

Missiuna, C. and Pollack, N. (1991) 'Play deprivation in children with physical disabilities: The role of the occupational therapist in preventing secondary disability', *American Journal of Occupational Therapy* **45**, 882–88.

Montague, S. (1997) *Man's Most Dangerous Myth: The Fallacy of Race*, 6th edn. Wallnut Break, USA: Alta Maria Press.

Montessori, M. (1964) *Reconstruction in Education*. Wheaton, IL: Theosophical Press.

Morley-Williams, L. M., O'Callaghan, J. and Cowie, H. (1995) 'Therapeutic issues in educational psychology: can attachment theory inform practice?', *Educational and Child Psychology* **12**(4), 48–54.

Moyles, J. R. (1988) *Just Playing? The Role and Status in Play in Early Childhood Education*. Milton Keynes: Open University Press.

Neppyl, T. K. and Murray, A. D. (1997) 'Social dominance and play patterns among pre-schoolers: gender comparisons'. *Sex Roles: A Journal of Research* **36**(5–6).

Newson, E. (1993) 'Play based assessment in the special needs classroom', in Harris, J. (ed.) *Innovations in Educating Children with Severe Learning Difficulties*. Chorley: Lisieux Hall.

Newton, C. (1988) '"Who knows me best?" Assessing pre-school children. Levels of participation in a child's world', *Educational Psychology in Practice* **3**(4), 35–9.

Parten, M. B. (1933) 'Social play amongst pre-school children', J*ournal of Abnormal and Social Psychology* **28**, 136–47.

Perner, J. (1991) *Understanding Representational Minds*. Cambridge, Mass: MIT.

Piaget, J. (1962) *Play, Dreams and Imitation in Childhood*. London: Routledge & Kegan Paul.

Piaget, J. (1964) 'Development and learning', in Ripple, R. E. and Rockcastle, V. N. (eds) *Piaget Rediscovered*. Conference on cognitive studies and curriculum development. Cornell University and University of California.

Piaget, J. (1966) 'Response to Brian Sutton-Smith', *Psychological Review*, 70, 111–12.

Quinn, J. and Rubin, K. (1984) 'The play of handicapped children', in Yawkey, T. D. and Pelligrini, A. (eds) *Child's Play: Developmental and Applied*. Hillsdale, NJ: Lawrence Erlbaum.

Resing, W. C. M. (1997) 'Learning potential assessment: the alternative for measuring intelligence?', *Educational and Child Psychology* **14**(4), 68–82.

Robinson, M. (1997) 'Supporting deaf children in the early years: an inclusive approach', in Wolfendale, S. (ed.) *Meeting Special Needs in the Early Years*. London: David Fulton Publishers.

Roopnarine, S., Lasker, J., Sacks, M. and Stores, M. (1998) 'The cultural contexts and children's play', in Saracho, O. and Spodek. B. (eds) *Multiple Perspectives on Play in Early Childhood Education*. Albany NY: Steele University. New York Press.

Rubin, K., Fein, G., Vandenburg, B. (1983). 'Play', in Mussen, P. H. (ed.) *Handbook of Child Psychology:* Vol. 4. *Socialisation, Personality and Social Behaviour.* New York: Wiley.

Saito, J. (1990) 'On Research of Study and Play', 11th IPA World Conference. Tokyo, June 1990.

Sayeed, Z. and Guerin, E. (1997) 'Play, assessment and culture', in Wolfendale, S. (ed.) *Meeting Special Needs in the Early Years.* London: David Fulton Publishers.

Schiller, V. *A History of Children's Play.* New Zealand 1840–1950 (cited in Sutton-Smith 1985).

Serbin, L. A., Sprafkin, C., Elman, M. and Doyle, M. B. (1982).'The early development of sex-differentiated patterns of social influence', *Canadian Journal of Social Science* **14**, 350–63.

Sheridan, M. D. (1977) *Spontaneous Play in Early Childhood from Birth to Six Years.* London: NFER Publishing Company.

Sigman, M. and Sena, R. (1993) 'Pretend play in high risk and developmentally delayed children', in Bornstein, M. H. and O'Reilly, A. W. (eds) *The role of play in the development of thought,* 29–42. San Francisco: Jossey-Bass.

Sinetar, M. (1991) *Developing a 21st Century Mind.* New York: Ballantine Books.

Singer, J. L and Singer, D. J. (1990) *The House of Make-believe: Children's Play and Developing Imagination.* Cambridge MA: Harvard University Press.

Skellenger, A. and Hill, E. W. (1994) 'Effects of shared teacher–child play intervention on the play skills of three young children who are blind', *Journal of Visual Impairment and Blindness* **88**(5) 433–45.

Skinner, B. G. (1953) *Science and Human Behaviour.* New York: Macmillan.

Smilansky, S. (1990) 'Socio-dramatic play: its relevance to behaviour and achievement in school', in Klugman, E. and Smilansky, S. *Children's Play and Learning: Perspectives and Policy Implications.* New York: Teachers' College Press.

Smith, P. K. and Cowie, H. (1991) *Understanding Children's Development,* 2nd edn. Oxford & Cambridge: Basil Blackwell.

Solity, J. (1993) 'Assessment through teaching: A case of mistaken identity', *Educational and Child Psychology* **10**(4), 27–46.

Spencer, H. (1878) *The Principles of Psychology.* New York: Appleton.

Sutton-Smith, B. (1966) 'Piaget on play: a critique', *Psychological Review* **73**, 104–10.

Sutton-Smith, B. (1985) 'The child at play', *Psychology Today,* October, 64–5.

Sutton-Smith, B. and Kelly-Byrne, D. (1986) ' The idealisation of play', in Smith, P. K. (ed.) *Play in Animals and Humans.* Oxford: Basil Blackwell.

Swedener, E. and John, J. (1989) 'Play in diverse social contexts: parents and teacher's roles', in Bloch, M. and Pelligrini, A. (eds) *The Ecological Context of Children's Play.* New York: Ablex.

Sylva, K., Roy, C. and Painter, M. (1980) 'Childwatching at playgroup and nursery school', *Oxford Pre-school Research Project.* Oxford: Grant McIntyre Blackwell.

Tait, P. (1973) 'Behaviour of young blind children in a controlled play setting', *Perception and Motor Skills* **34**, 963–69.

Takeuchi, M. (1994) 'Children's play in Japan', in Roopnarine, J., Johnson, J. and Hooper, F. (eds) *Children's Play in Diverse Cultures*, 51–72. Albany, NY: State University of New York Press.

Thorne, B. (1993) *Gender Play – Boys and Girls in School*. Milton Keynes: Open University Press.

Trickey, G. (1993) 'Measurement technology UK: Fad, fashion and phoenix in assessment issues', *Educational and Child Psychology* **10**(4), 7–13.

Trumbell, D. (1990) 'Introduction', in Duckworth, E., Eastley, J., Hawkins, D. and Henriques, A. (eds) *Science Education: A Minds-on Approach for the Elementary Years*. Hillsdale, NJ: Lawrence Erlbaum Associates.

Tzuriel, D. (1996) 'Mediated learning experience in free-play versus structured situations among pre-school, low, medium and high schools', *Child Development and Care* **126**, 57–82.

Tzuriel, D. (1997) 'Learning and Instruction'. Pre-publication copy. Binot Centre, London.

Tzuriel, D. (1997) 'A novel dynamic assessment approach for young children: major dimensions and current research', *Educational and Child Psychology* **14**(5), 83–107.

Valett, R. E. (1983) 'Strategies for developing creative imagination and thinking skills', in Boyer, W.A.R. (1997) 'Playfulness enhancement through classroom intervention', *Childhood Education* **74**(2), 90.

Vygotsky, L. (1967) 'Play and its role in the mental development of the child', *Soviet Psychology* **12**(6), 62–76.

Vygotsky, L. S. (1978) *Mind in Society: The development of Higher Psychological Processes*. Edited translation by Cole, M., John, M., Steiner, V., Scribner, S. and Saubsman, E. Cambridge, MA: MIT Press.

Waite, V. and Wood, K. (1999) 'Educational psychologists' assessment of autism', *Educational Psychology in Practice* **15**(3), 167–44.

Walker, A. (1997) *Anything We Have Can Be Saved*. London: The Women's Press.

Waters, J. (1999) *Let's Play: A Guide to Interactive Assessment with Young Children*. Newcastle City Council.

Waters, J. and Stringer, P. (1997) 'The bunny bag: a dynamic approach to the assessment of pre-school children', *Educational and Child Psychology. Innovative Approaches to Dynamic Assessment* **14**(4), 33–44.

White, M. (1997) 'A review of the influence and effects of Portage', in Wolfendale, S. (ed.) *Working with Parents of SEN Children after the Code of Practice*. London: David Fulton Publishers.

White, M. and Cameron, R. J. (1987) *Portage Early Education Programme – A Practical Manual*. Windsor: NFER-Nelson.

Whiting, B. and Whiting, J. (1975) *Children of Six*. Cambridge, MA: Harvard University Press.

Whiting, B. B. and Edwards, C. P. (1988) *Children of Different Worlds*. Cambridge, MA: Harvard University Press.

Wing, L., Gould, J., Yeates, S. R. and Brierly, L. M. (1977) 'Symbolic play in mentally retarded and autistic children', *Journal of Child Psychology and Psychiatry* **18**, 167–78.

Winnicott, D. W. (1971) *Playing and Reality*. London: Tavistock.

Winnicott, D. W. (1990) *Playing and Reality*. London: Routledge.

Winter, S. M., Bell, M. J. and Dempsey, J. D. (1994) 'Creating play environments for children with special needs', *Childhood Education* **71**(1), 28–33.

Wolfendale, S. (1993) *Assessing Special Educational Needs*. London: Cassell.

Wolfendale, S. (1998) *All About Me*, 2nd edn. Nottingham: NES Arnold.

Wood, E. and Attfield, J. (1996) *Play, Learning and Early Childhood Curriculum*. London: Paul Chapman Publishing.

# Index